Biography

James Egan was born in 1985 and grew up in Portarlington, Co. Laois in the Midlands of Ireland.
In 2008, James moved to England and studied in Oxford.
James married his wife in 2012 and currently lives in Havant in Hampshire.
James had his first book, 365 Ways to Stop Sabotaging Your Life, published in 2014.
Several of James' books have become No.1 Best Sellers in the UK including 1000 Facts about Horror Movies, 3000 Facts About the Greatest Movies Ever, 365 Things People Believe That Aren't True, Another 365 Things People Believe That Aren't True, and 500 Things People Believe That Aren't True.

Books by James Egan

Fairytale
Inherit the Earth
Inherit the Earth: The Animal Kingdom
1000 Facts About the United States
Words That Need to Exist in English
Hilarious Things That Kids Say
Hilarious Things That Mums Say
1000 Facts about TV Shows Vol. 1-3
1000 Facts about Animated Shows Vol. 1-3
1000 Facts about Actors Vol. 1-3
1000 Facts about Countries Vol. 1-3
Dinosaurs Had Feathers (and other Random Facts)
1000 Facts about Animals Vol. 1-3
1000 Facts about James Bond
1000 Inspiring Facts
How to Psychologically Survive Cancer
1000 Out-of-this-World Facts about Space
1000 Facts about the Greatest Movies Ever Vol. 1-3
1000 Facts about Film Directors
1000 Facts about Superhero Movies Vol. 1-3
1000 Facts about Superheroes Vol. 1-3
1000 Facts about Supervillains Vol. 1-3
1000 Facts about Comic Books Vol. 1-3
1000 Facts about Animated Films Vol. 1-3
1000 Facts about Horror Movies Vol. 1-3
1000 Facts about American Presidents
Adorable Animal Facts
1000 Facts about Video Games Vol. 1-3
Things People Believe That Aren't True Vol. 1-4
1000 Fact about Film Director
The Mega Misconception Book
3000 Astounding Quotes
1000 Facts About Comic Book Characters Vol. 1-3
100 Classic Stories in 100 Pages
500 Facts about Godzilla
365 Ways to Stop Sabotaging Your Life
Flat Earthers Around the Globe
1000 Facts about Historic Figures Vol. 1-3
1000 Facts About Writers
1000 Facts about Ireland
The Biggest Movie Plotholes
1000 Facts about the Human Body

1000 Facts about Animated Films Vol. 3

By

James Egan

Copyright 2016 © James Egan

All rights reserved. No part of this book may be reproduced, stored, or transmitted by any means - whether auditory, graphic, mechanical, or electronic - without written permission of both publisher and author, except in the case of brief excerpts used in critical articles and reviews. Unauthorized reproduction of any part of this work is illegal and is punishable by law.

ISBN: 978-0-244-03014-8

Because of the dynamic nature of the Internet, any web addresses or links contained in this book may have changed since publication and may no longer be valid. The views expressed in this work are solely those of the author and do not necessarily reflect the views of the publisher, and the publisher hereby disclaims any responsibility for them.

Any people depicted in stock imagery provided by Thinkstock are models, and such images are being used for illustrative purposes only.
Certain stock imagery © Thinkstock.

Lulu Publishing Services rev. date: 01/09/2017

*Dedicated to
Stacey Thorncroft*

Contents

A Goofy Movie	p9
The Addams Family	p10
The Adventures of Ichabod and Mr. Toad	p12
The Adventures of Tintin	p14
Akira	p16
Aladdin	p18
Alice in Wonderland	p20
All Dogs Go to Heaven	p22
Anastasia	p23
Animal Farm	p24
The Animatrix	p25
Atlantis: The Lost Empire	p27
Balto	p29
Bambi	p31
Beauty and the Beast	p33
Bee Movie	p36
The BFG	p37
The Black Cauldron	p38
Bolt	p39
Book of Life	p40
The Boxtrolls	p41
Brave	p42
Brother Bear	p43
Captain Underpants: The First Epic Movie	p44
Castle in the Sky	p45
Chicken Little	p46
Cinderella	p47
Cloudy with a Chance of Meatballs	p49
Coco	p50
The Croods	p52
Ferdinand	p54
Ferngully: The Last Rainforest	p56
Final Fantasy VII: Advent Children	p57
Final Fantasy: The Spirits Within	p58
Finding Nemo	p60
Flushed Away	p63

Foodfight!	p64
The Fox and the Hound	p66
Frankenweenie	p67
Frozen	p68
Fun & Fancy Free	p71
Ghost in the Shell	p72
Hercules	p73
Howl's Moving Castle	p75
The Incredibles	p76
Inside Out	p79
The Iron Giant	p81
The Jungle Book	p83
Klaus	p85
Kubo and the Two Strings	p86
Kung Fu Panda	p87
The Lego Movie	p88
The Lion King	p90
The Little Mermaid	p92
The Lorax	p94
The Lord of the Rings	p95
Mary and Max	p96
Meet the Robinsons	p97
Megamind	p98
Minions	p99
Moana	p100
Monsters vs Aliens	p101
Mr. Peabody & Sherman	p102
Nausicaa of the Valley of the Wind	p103
The Nightmare Before Christmas	p104
The Pirates! Band of Misfits	p106
Pocahontas	p107
Pokémon: The First Movie – Mewtwo Strikes Back	p108
The Prince of Egypt	p109
Ralph Breaks the Internet	p110
Rio	p112
Rise of the Guardians	p113
Robots	p114

The Secret of NIMH	p115
Shark Tale	p116
Shaun the Sheep Movie	p117
A Shaun the Sheep Movie: Farmageddon	p118
Shrek	p119
Shrek 2	p121
The Simpsons Movie	p123
Sinbad: Legend of the Seven Seas	p124
Sleeping Beauty	p125
Smallfoot	p127
Smurfs: The Lost Village	p128
Snow White and the Seven Dwarves	p129
Spirited Away	p131
Spirit: Stallion of the Cimarron	p132
The SpongeBob SquarePants Movie	p133
The SpongeBob Movie: Sponge Out of Water	p134
The SpongeBob Movie: Sponge on the Run	p135
Street Fighter II: The Animated Movie	p136
The Sword in the Stone	p137
Tangled	p138
Tarzan	p140
TMNT	p141
The Thief and the Cobbler	p142
The Three Caballeros	p144
Toy Story	p145
Toy Story 2	p147
Toy Story 3	p149
Toy Story 4	p150
Up	p152
Wallace and Gromit: Curse of the Were-Rabbit	p153
WALL-E	p154
Zootopia	p155

A Goofy Movie
1995

1. The CEO of Disney, Jeffrey Katzenberg, was working so hard during the 1990s, he barely saw his daughter.
    This encouraged him to make a film about a father taking a road trip with his child to bring them closer together. This concept turned into A Goofy Movie.

2. Rob Paulsen voices Pete's son, PJ. He has never seen the film.

3. Steve Martin was considered for the role of Goofy.

4. In the original script, Goofy and Max were going to compete on a game show called America's Funniest Gladiators.

5. Donald Duck was supposed to play a pivotal role as a travel agent.

6. Originally, Pete was going to play a more significant role. He would be on a road trip in a gigantic truck, taunting Goofy everywhere he goes. This concept was taken from Steven Spielberg's film, Duel.

7. The tagline is "It's the story of a father who couldn't be closer... to driving his son crazy."

8. Bizarrely, The Lion King was supposed to come out in 1995 and A Goofy Movie was going to come out in 1994.
    When A Goofy Movie was delayed, The Lion King was rushed for release a year early. That's right. The Lion King came out a year early and it's STILL the best Disney film ever!

The Addams Family
2019

9. The story was inspired by a comic strip created by Charles Addams. Most of the characters in the comic strip were unnamed.

10. Fester barely appeared in the comic.

11. Wednesday Addams' name references the nursery rhyme, Wednesday's Child is Full of Woe.

12. Gomez was originally going to be called Repelli. Pugsley was going to be called Pubert.

13. Snoop Dogg provides the voice of Cousin Itt.

14. Oscar Isaac provides the voice of Gomez. Charlize Theron provides the voice of Morticia. Although they play a married couple, the actors didn't meet until after the film wrapped.

15. As soon as the trailer was released, viewers criticised Gomez's horrid appearance since the character is depicted as handsome in previous films and television series.
    However, every character in the film is based on their designs in the original comics. Gomez's appearance is based on Peter Lorre who played Cairo in The Maltese Falcon.
    Morticia is modelled off Gloria Swanson, who played Norma in Sunset Blvd.

16. The tree is called Ichabod. It is named after the main character in Sleepy Hollow, Ichabod Crane.

17. Wednesday's pigtails are shaped like nooses.

18. This is the first animated adaption where Pugsley is voiced by a child.

19. The film was meant to be in stop-motion.

20. In Mexico, Thing's name is Fingers, Gomez is called Homero, Uncle Fester is called Lucas, Pugsley is called Pericles, and Wednesday is called Merlina.

The Adventures of Ichabod and Mr. Toad
1949

21. The film is split into two parts; The first part revolves around Mr. Toad from The Wind in the Willows.
    The second part revolves around Ichabod Crane from The Legend of Sleepy Hollow.

22. The Legend of Sleepy Hollow takes place in 1790. The Wind in the Willows takes place in 1909-1910.

23. The Headless Horseman is so scary, Disney still receive complaints about him to this day.

24. J. Pat O' Malley voices Cyril. O' Malley also voices Jasper in 101 Dalmatians and Hathi in The Jungle Book.

25. It took eight years to make this film.

26. The film was nearly called Two Fabulous Characters.

27. Ichabod's horse is called Gunpowder.

28. Ichabod Crane's body is designed to look like a crane bird.

29. Ichabod is named after a Biblical character. In the Bible, Ichabod is said to mean "inglorious" because he was born on a day of military defeat.

30. Ichabod Crane is described as looking like a scarecrow. Ichabod was the inspiration for the Batman supervillain, the Scarecrow. Scarecrow's real name is Jonathan Crane.

31. Basil Rathbone narrates Toad's story. He is best-known for playing Sherlock Holmes in over ten films during the 1940s.

32. Brom Bones' real name is Abraham Van Brunt. He is named after the Biblical character, Abraham. "Abraham" means "exalted father."

33. Brom Bones inspired the character of Gaston in Beauty and the Beast.

The Adventures of Tintin:
The Secret of the Unicorn
2011

34. The story takes place in 1955.

35. Steven Spielberg intended the film to be live action. When he contacted Peter Jackson to see if he could use his special effects team, Jackson convinced Spielberg that the film couldn't work in live action. The directors decided to team up to make a computer-generated Tintin film.

36. Roman Polanski wanted to direct the film.

37. Daniel Craig plays Red Rackham. Toby Jones plays Silk. Both of them worked together in Infamous.

38. The film cost $135 million. Although the director thought the film would be a major success, it only made $374 million, which was considered a small profit. The film didn't do well in the US since the comics are not very well-known outside Europe.

39. Steven Spielberg always looks at his scenes with one eye closed to visualise the image in 2D. He didn't do this with this film because it is in 3D.

40. Many directors including Robert Zemeckis, David Fincher, and James Cameron visited the set.

41. Simon Pegg and Nick Frost play Thompson and Thomson. Both actors worked together in Shaun of the Dead, Hot Fuzz, and The World's End.

42. It only took Spielberg 31 days to shoot the film.

43. Peter Jackson stood in for Haddock during test-screening. Spielberg thought Jackson was an excellent Haddock.

Akira
1988

44. The film is based on a 2,500-page manga comic book. Since the comic is so gigantic, the film only deals with a very small portion of the story.

45. 50 colours were used for Akira that had never been used for an animated film.

46. The main character is called Kanaeda. In the Japanese version, his name is pronounced "Canada." It's pronounced "Ka-nay-da" in the English dub because Western viewers found it silly that the main character's name sounded like the country, Canada.

47. The manga was so successful, it was translated into English by Marvel Comics. This is one of the first times in history that a non-English comic series was completely translated into English.

48. This was directed by Katsuhiro Otomo. He was the writer of the original manga.

49. This was the most expensive animated film made at the time in Japan, costing $10 million.

50. The Wachowski brothers said Akira was the biggest influence for their film, The Matrix. When Akira was re-released in 2001, its tagline was, "No Akira, No Matrix."

51. The film was released two years after the manga concluded.

52. The film had 738 storyboard pages. The director also wrote 2,000 pages worth of ideas.

53. Leonardo DiCaprio bought the rights to make a live-action version of the story.

54. The film contains 2,212 shots and 160,000 single pictures, which is three times more than an average animated film.

Aladdin
1992

55. In an early script, there were two Genies; one Genie was in a lamp and the other was in a ring. In this version, the Genie could grant infinite wishes.

56. The original script was written by Linda Woolverton. Woolverton wrote the screenplay for Beauty and the Beast.

57. The Carpet was difficult to animate since it couldn't display emotion with speech or facial expressions. The animators studied Charlie Chaplin to learn how a character displays emotion without talking.

58. The director said that Jafar was based on the former First Lady, Nancy Reagan.

59. In the original script, Aladdin recognised Jasmine as the princess as soon as he saw her. This was changed as the writers thought it would be better if Aladdin fell in love with her, not knowing of her heritage.

60. When the Genie frees Aladdin from the Cave of Wonders, Genie calls him "Mr Doubting Mustafa." This is a reference to the idiom "doubting Thomas." Also, Mustafa is the name of Aladdin's father in the original story.

61. During the Genie's song, he mentions Ali Baba and the Forty Thieves. The second sequel, Aladdin and the King of Thieves, revolves around this legend.

62. Jasmine's character is the opposite of how she was depicted in the original script. In the first draft, Jasmine

was a spoilt brat who wanted to find the richest prince possible.

63. During the Whole New World scene, Aladdin and Jasmine fly over Japan and Greece. The designs of the buildings were used again for the films, Hercules and Mulan.

64. Robin Williams had a massive falling out with Disney and he refused to return for the sequel, The Return of Jafar.

   Disney eventually apologised to Robin Williams and he agreed to return as the Genie in the sequel, Aladdin and the King of Thieves.

65. The film spawned a television show in 1994. Since Robin Williams didn't want anything to do with it, Dan Castellaneta voices the Genie. Castellaneta is most famous for voicing Homer Simpson in The Simpsons.

66. In the original script, the story revolved around Aladdin's relationship with his mother. She desperately wanted Aladdin to stop living as a thief but he kept getting encouraged by his friends.

Alice in Wonderland
1951

67.   The only character that is in the original story that wasn't in the film was Mock Turtle. The Doorknob is the only character in the film that wasn't in the original story.

68.   Lewis Carroll's real name is Charles Lutwidge Dodgson.

69.   Kathryn Beaumont was 13 when she voiced Alice in this film. She reprised her role in the video game, Kingdom Hearts, over half a century later.

70.   The Dodo is based on Lewis Carroll. Like Carroll, the Dodo has a stutter in the novel. When Carroll said his surname, it sounded like "Dodogson."

71.   Lewis Carroll wrote a poem called Jabberwocky which revolved around a monster called the Jabberwock. Although it was supposed to appear in this film, it was scrapped as Disney thought the monster was too scary.

72.   The Queen of Hearts in the film is based on the character of the same name in Alice's Adventures in Wonderland and The Red Queen in Through the Looking Glass.

73.   The March Hare is called Haigha.

74.   The Drink Me bottle was originally going to speak.

75.   Alice changes in size when she drinks or eats certain things in Wonderland. Lewis Carroll came up with this idea while he suffered from migraines.

Sometimes his headaches were so severe, objects looked smaller or larger than they were.

76.   Lewis Carroll didn't invent the Cheshire Cat character. The phrase "grins like a Cheshire cat" has been found in a 1788 dictionary.

All Dogs Go to Heaven
1989

77. The film was made by Don Bluth. He used to be a Disney animator.

78. The title is based on a quote by Robert Louis Stevenson, "You think those dogs will not be in heaven? I tell you they will be there long before any of us."

79. Burt Reynolds voices the lead, Charlie B. Barkin.

80. Judith Barsi voices the female lead, Anne-Marie. She was murdered shortly after she recorded her lines. She was only ten years old when she was killed.

81. Near the end of the film, a big-lipped alligator called King Gator suddenly appears with no explanation. He doesn't fit the context of the story nor does he advance the plot.
    When YouTube vlogger, The Nostalgia Critic, discussed this scene, he coined the term, Big Lipped Alligator Moment when referencing a movie scene that comes out of nowhere. The term, Big Lipped Alligator moment, is now often used to reference nonsensical scenes in movies.

Anastasia
1997

82. "Anastasia" means "resurrection."

83. The puppy is called Pooka. In Irish mythology, a pooka is a shape-shifter that brings good luck.

84. Christopher Lloyd voices Rasputin. The character was nearly voiced by Tim Curry, Jonathan Pryce, and Patrick Stewart.

85. During the song, Learn to Do It, someone mentions Uncle Vanya. Uncle Vanya is a popular play in Russia written by Anton Chekhov.

86. Kelsey Grammar voices Vlad. This is the first animated film he worked on.

87. The director didn't like the final design of Vlad.

88. Meg Ryan voices Anastasia. Kirsten Dunst voices her as a young girl.

89. Angela Lansbury voices Empress Marie.

90. Jim Cummings provides Rasputin's singing voice. Cummings is so good at imitating Christopher Lloyd's voice, most people don't realise it's sung by a different person.

Animal Farm
1954

91. The film is based on George Orwell's novel which was published in 1945. The head of the CIA, E. Howard Hunt, bought the film rights from Orwell's widow, Sonia.
Hunt was directly involved in the Watergate scandal that forced Richard Nixon to resign from the American presidency.

92. Sonia Orwell only agreed to sell the rights under the condition that she could meet her idol, Clark Gable.

93. In the original novel, the pigs betray the other animals and join forces with the humans. This ending was considered too depressing so it was changed.

94. This was the first British animated film ever.

95. Maurice Denham voices every character.

The Animatrix
2003

96. This film revolves around the origins of the background and sides-stories of The Matrix. The film was released several weeks after The Matrix Reloaded.

97. The Animatrix is made of nine shorts –
i) The Second Renaissance Part I – A summary of how the machines turned against humanity.
ii) The Second Renaissance Part II – A summary of how the machines built The Matrix.
iii) Kid's Story – A tale about the first person who consciously exited the Matrix.
iv) A Detective Story – A private detective is tasked with tracking down the computer hacker, Trinity.
v) Final Flight of the Osiris – A 3D short that shows what happened to the crew who discovered the army of Squiddies drilling to Zion.
vi) Program – A man who lives in Zion who decides to return to living inside The Matrix.
vii) Beyond – A group of kids discover an area that "glitches" in The Matrix.
viii) World Record – An athlete commits an unprecedented incident by running faster than he physically should be capable of by bending the rules of The Matrix program.
ix) Matriculated – A resistance group tries to reprogram a sentinel.

98. In The Matrix Reloaded, one of the main Zionists is referred to as Kid. In Kid's Story, it is revealed that his name is Michael Popper.

99. The Final Flight of the Osiris takes place moments before The Matrix Reloaded begins.

100. Tom Kenny voices the Operator. Kenny voices the titular character in the animated series, SpongeBob Squarepants.

101. The Name Plate on the Osiris reads, "Mark IV 16: OSIRIS: Made in the USA 2097." In the Bible, Mark IV 16 reads, "John, the man I beheaded, has been raised from the Dead." Osiris was the Egyptian god of the afterlife and could raise mortals back from the dead.

102. The tagline is "Free your mind."

103. In The Matrix, Morpheus tells Neo that it is unknown whether the humans or the machines struck first.

It is revealed in The Second Renaissance Part I, that a servant robot kills his owners after he learned they were going to dispose of him for a better model. To ensure this didn't happen again, humanity discontinued this model permanently.

When a pair of robots made a peace offering to The United Nations to show that they bared no ill will to humanity, the machines were detained. The machines saw this rejection as an act of war. This began the war between humanity and the machines.

Atlantis:
The Lost Empire
2001

104. Marc Okrand created the Atlantean language. He also invented the Vulcan and Klingon languages in Star Trek. Speaking of which…

105. Leonard Nimoy voices King Kashekim. He's best-known for playing Spock in Star Trek.

106. The crew wore t-shirts that read, "Fewer songs, more explosions."

107. This is one of the only Disney films that says what year it takes place in – 1914.

108. This was directed by Gary Trousedale and Kirk Wise. They also directed Beauty and the Beast and The Hunchback of Notre Dame.

109. Kida is the first Disney princess to become a queen.

110. The animators thought it was clichéd to design Atlantis as "crumbled Greek columns underwater." Because of this, they drew Atlantis so it resembled Mayan buildings.

111. Milo mentions that Shepherd's journal suddenly stops as if there's a page missing. This is a reference to Plato's stories, Timaeus and Critias, where the story cuts off, as if the rest of the pages have been ripped out.

112. The tagline is "In a single day and night of misfortune, the island of Atlantis disappeared into the

depths of the sea." This quote is from Plato, who devised the story of Atlantis.

113.   Disney made three episodes of an Atlantis series. When the series wasn't picked up, Disney decided to turn the three episodes into the sequel, Atlantis: Milo's Return.

Balto
1995

114. The film is based on the true story of a husky called Balto who led his team to a village called Nome. The inhabitants were gripped with diphtheria and desperately needed to be inoculated. When Balto reached Nome, the team inoculated the people with an antitoxin. Balto is perceived as a hero since his actions led to an entire town being saved.

    However, Balto did not run the longest part nor the most hazardous part of the journey. Of the 20 mushers on this journey, Seppala's husky, Togo, ran further than any other dog on the expedition, at a staggering 260 miles. The reason why Balto got the credit is because he ran the final 55 miles.

    Seppala was so angry that his dog didn't receive credit for the expedition that he didn't invite Balto or his owner to Togo's award ceremony in New York.

115. In the film, Balto is a wolf hybrid. In real life, Balto was a purebred Siberian husky.

116. Kevin Bacon voices Balto.

117. Phil Collins voices Muk and Luk. They are named after a type of Canadian shoe called mukluks.

118. The film spawned the sequels, Balto: Wolf Quest and Balto III: Wings of Change.

119. The tagline is "Part dog. Part wolf. All hero."

120. Although the film received positive reviews, it tanked at the box office because it came out the same time as Toy Story.

121. The Serum Run that Balto committed is known as the Iditarod.

122. Balto doesn't speak in the last 15 minutes of the film.

Bambi
1942

123. This was the first Disney film where none of the songs were sung by any of the characters.

124. The film was cleaned up when it was released on DVD. Many viewers don't understand how much work it takes to clean up the negatives of an old film. Disney filmmakers spent 9,600 hours cleaning the negatives (over a year) to make them look as sharp as possible.

125. Originally, Bambi was going to be shot, not his mother.

126. Originally, Bambi was supposed to run up to his dead mother after she is shot.

127. Walt Disney decided not to show the hunter as he worried that children would assume all hunters are evil.

128. Donnie Dunagan voices Young Bambi. He became a Marine and the youngest drill instructor in history and eventually became a Major in the Vietnam War. He never told anyone that he voiced Bambi during the war, afraid that he would get bullied.

129. The original story is considered to be one of the first environmental novels.

130. The film cost $1.7 million. The film only made $1.64 million at the box office. The film didn't do well because it wasn't released in Japan or Europe for years due to WWII. This was the last animated Disney film for eight years because most of animators were in the military during the war.

131. The animation from this film has been recycled more than any other Disney cartoon. Shots of birds flying, leaves blowing, forest animals sleeping, etc. have been used in other films including The Sword in the Stone, The Jungle Book, and The Rescuers.

132. Bambi II was released in 2006. This means there is a gap of 64 years between the original and the sequel, which is the world record.

133. When America Film Institute ranked the 100 greatest heroes and villains, the murderer of Bambi's mother (simply known as Man,) was ranked #20. He was the only person on the list that never appeared onscreen.

Beauty and the Beast
1991

134. The film inspired a spin-off in 1997 called Beauty and the Beast: The Enchanted Christmas.

135. When Beast gets a makeover, he says that he looks stupid. His look in this scene is based on the Cowardly Lion from The Wizard of Oz.

136. The film had another spin-off film in 1998 called Belle's Magical World. It was supposed to be an animated series but it was cancelled after three episodes due to poor animation and storylines. The studio decided to repackage it as a movie to make some money back. It is considered to be the worst animated Disney movie ever.

137. Jerry Orbach voices Lumiere. He played Lennie in Law & Order for 13 years.

138. Richard White voices Gaston. He only has five acting credits.

139. This is one of the first films that Pixar worked on. They animated the chandelier during Belle and Beast's dance.

140. Although most animated films take four or five years to make, Beauty and the Beast only took two years.

141. The song, Human Again, was completed but not used for the finished film. It was inserted into the movie when it was released on DVD.

142. Tony Jay voices the owner of the insane asylum, Monsier D'Arque. The filmmakers said he performed the best audition. He was so good, the director used his audition for the final film so Jay didn't have come in to voice any additional dialogue.

143. Belles final dance with the Prince is recycled animation from Princess Aurora and Prince Phillip in the film, Sleeping Beauty.

144. This was the most successful film of the year apart from Terminator 2.

145. The Beast's appearance is a composition of many animals. He has a bear's body, a boar's tusks, a lion's main, a gorilla's brow, a buffalo's beard, a human's eyes, and a wolf's tail and legs.

146. The earliest version of this story is Cupid and Psyche, which was written in the 2nd century by Platonicus. The main character, Lucius, transmogrifies into a donkey after a magic spell goes wrong. He regains his humanity after eating a sacred rose.

147. Another version of the Beauty and the Beast was The Pig King, which was written by Gianfrancesco in the 16th century. The story revolves around a mother who urges her daughters to marry a king called Marcassin. Although the daughters are repulsed by Marcassin because he resembles a boar-beast, the mother begs one of them to marry him for his money. This story was written to show the pressure that people in arranged marriages go through.

148. The most famous version of Beauty and the Beast is the 1756 tale by Jeanne-Marie Leprince de Beaumont. However, there are many differences between this

version and the Disney film. In Beaumont's story, the Beast is kind from the very beginning. He does not entice the girl (who is called Beauty) in any way and does not sit with her unless she asks him to. The Beast believes a person of purity will love him for his kindness rather than his appearance.

Bee Movie
2007

149. Barry and other male bees have stingers. In real life, only female bees have stingers. Also, bees don't make honey in real life.

150. Jerry Seinfeld voices the lead, Barry B. Benson. The role nearly went to Jason Bateman.

151. Jerry Seinfeld came up with the title as a joke to Steven Spielberg. Spielberg loved the idea and encouraged Seinfeld to make it into a film.

152. Renee Zellweger voices Vanessa. Jennifer Lopez was considered for the role.

153. The story was originally going to be live-action.

154. The film inspired a rip-off called Plan Bee, which came out the same year.

155. Sting, Ray Liotta, and Larry King voice themselves.

156. The tagline is, "Honey just got funny."

157. The first trailer was in live-action and has Jerry Seinfeld dressed in a bee costume.

158. John Goodman voices Layton. The role nearly went to James Gandolfini.

159. Buzzwell is modelled after The Boss from the animated series, Dilbert.

The BFG
1989

160. The film is based on the 1982 book of the same name. When the writer, Roald Dahl, saw this film, he said he enjoyed it. This is pretty impressive since he detested the film Willie Wonka and the Chocolate Factory, which was based on his novel, Charlie and the Chocolate Factory.

161. The film was first shown on Christmas Day in 1989 in the UK.

162. David Jason voices the titular character.

163. David Jason named his daughter, Sophie. Sophie is the name of the main character in this story.

164. The boy who dreams of turning invisible has a Danger Mouse poster in his bedroom. David Jason played the titular character in the cartoon, Danger Mouse.

The Black Cauldron
1985

165. This was the first animated Disney film to have no songs.

166. Disney studios tried to make the film since 1971.

167. John Hurt voices the main villain, the Horned King.

168. The film was suspended from video release for years because it was considered too disturbing for children.

169. This is the film that Disney is most ashamed of.

170. Tim Burton was one of the crewmembers. He wanted the Horned King to have lackeys that resembled the Facehuggers from the Alien series.

171. The Horned King's demise is considered to be the most horrific death in any Disney film.

172. It took 12 years to make this film.

173. This was the first Disney film to use the iconic Disney logo in the beginning.

Bolt
2008

174. The story revolves around a dog called Bolt who stars in a TV show about a canine with superpowers. However, Bolt actually believes he has superpowers and becomes incredibly confused and disillusioned when he gets lost.

    The film's structure was heavily inspired by The Truman Show, which also revolved around a character who was unaware that he is the star of a show.

175. In Russia, the film is called Volt. In Poland, the film is called Lightning. In Bulgaria, the film is called Thunder.

176. The Bolt TV show was supposed to be called The Omega Dog.

177. The short, Tokyo Mater, was shown in the cinema before this film.

178. The tagline is "Fully awesome."

179. John Travolta voices the titular character.

180. James Lipton voices The Director. Lipton is the host of Inside the Actors Studio.

181. Malcolm McDowell voices the feline-themed villain, Dr. Calico. A calico is a type of cat.

182. This was the first film ever released on Blu-Ray before DVD.

Book of Life
2014

183. Channing Tatum voices Joaquin. Ice Cube voices Candle Maker. They worked together in 21 Jump Street.

184. The original title was El Matador.

185. Ron Perlman voices Xibalba. Xibalba is the name of the Underworld according to the Ancient Mayans.

186. Christian Applegate voices Mary Beth. She is best-known for playing Kelly in Married with Children and Veronica in Anchorman.

187. The film is called Day of the Dead in the United States.

The Boxtrolls
2014

188.   Simon Pegg voices Herbert. Nick Frost voices Trout. The pair have worked together on many projects including Spaced and Shaun of the Dead.
Weirdly, they had no idea that the other was in the film because they recorded their lines separately.

189.   20,000 props were made for the film.

190.   Dee Bradley Baker voices Fish, Wheels, and Bucket. He's one of the best voice actors in the world and has starred in over 450 projects. He also helped developed the boxtroll language.

191.   Elle Fanning voices Winnie. Her sister, Dakota, was the lead of Coraline, which was made by the same stop-motion company, Laika.

192.   330 stop-motion animators worked on the film.

193.   The tagline was, "Heroes come in all shapes and sizes… even rectangles."

Brave
2012

194. John Ratzenberg voices Gordon. He has starred in nearly 20 Pixar films.

195. Billy Connolly voices Fergus. Sean Connery was considered for the role.

196. "Merida" is Hebrew for "rebel."

197. Julie Walters voices the Witch. David Tennant was considered for the role.

198. Robbie Coltrane voices Lord Dingwall. Kelly Macdonald voices Merida. Both actors worked on the Harry Potter series.

199. The black bear is called Mor'du. It is based on the Gaelic term, "Mor Dubh," which means "large black one."

200. There is a theory that the witch is actually Boo from Monsters, Inc. Now you might think, "That doesn't make any sense! Boo is a toddler in Monsters, Inc. and Brave is set centuries ago! How could you possibly connect the two?"
    Because the witch has a carving of Boo's friend, Sulley. The theory suggests that Boo becomes a witch when she becomes older and eventually time-travels to medieval Scotland where she meets Merida.

Brother Bear
2003

201. Rick Moranis voices Rutt in this film and the 2006 sequel. He's best-known for Ghostbusters, Spaceballs, and Honey, I Shrunk the Kids. Brother Bear 2 is the last film he has starred in.

202. Joaquin Phoenix voices the lead, Kenai.

203. The moose are called Tuke and Rutt. In the German version, they are called Benny and Bjorn. They are named after the two male singers from the Swedish band, ABBA.

204. The tagline is, "The Moose Are Loose!"

205. Disney considered making a spin-off show of Tuke and Rutt.

206. Most of the characters are named after places in Alaska.

207. Michael Clarke Duncan voices Tug the bear. He played a character called Bear in Armageddon. Tug's appearance and facial expressions were modelled after Michael Clark Duncan.

Captain Underpants:
The First Epic Movie
2017

208. The story is based on Dav Pilkey's book series, The Adventures of Captain Underpants. The series ran from 1997-2015.

209. The film was supposed to be made in the early 2000s with Chris Farley voicing the titular character. After Farley died, the project was shelved.

210. The story is based on the first four books.

211. The tagline was, "Putting the Mighty in Tighty Whitey."

212. Kevin Hart voices George. Ed Helms voices Captain Underpants. They worked together before in the 2008 film, Meet Dave.

Castle in the Sky
1986

213. The story takes place in the floating castle of Laputa. It's named after the flying island in Jonathan Swift's novel, Gulliver's Travels.

214. The film was originally in Japanese. It wasn't dubbed into English for 13 years.

215. Shita's name was changed to Sheeta for the English dub for… obvious reasons.

216. This was the first film created by Studio Ghibli.

217. Mark Hamill voices Muska.

218. The title was Laputa but it was changed when the director learned that it translated into "slag" in Spanish.

Chicken Little
2005

219. When Buck Cluck is driving Chicken Little to school, a bull can be seen in a China shop.

220. Patrick Stewart voices Mr. Woolensworth. This is the first Disney film that Stewart has been a part of. He was offered nine other Disney roles in other Disney films but he was busy shooting Star Trek.

221. Mark Dindal directed the film. He also directed The Emperor's New Groove.

222. The tagline is "Who you calling chicken?"

223. The first few minutes of the story is based on the fable, The Sky is Falling.

224. Zach Braff voices the titular role.

225. Chicken Little was going to be a girl.

226. Adam West voices Ace.

Cinderella
1950

227. Cinderella was the first Disney princess not to be born into royalty.

228. June Foray voices Lucifer the cat. She also voices Betty in The Flintstones.

229. When Cinderella dances with Prince Charming, their shadows don't match. This is because the animators found it too difficult.

230. The tagline is "The greatest love story ever told."

231. The film spawned a sequel in 2002 called Cinderella II: Dreams Come True.
    The film had another sequel in 2007 called Cinderella 3: A Twist in Time. In this film, Cinderella's evil step-mother, Lady Tremaine, goes back in time to make sure Cinderella never becomes a princess.

232. Although Cinderella was nominated for three Oscars, the film didn't win anything.

233. When the Fairy Godmother performs her magic spell on Cinderella, a halo appears above Cinderella's head for a split-second.

234. There is an urban legend that the slippers were made of squirrel fur in one of the original stories but this isn't true.

235. The mice's clothes are similar to the dwarves from Snow White and the Seven Dwarfs. Gus' clothes and hat are the same colour as Bashful the Dwarf.

236. This is not the first Cinderella cartoon made by Disney. Walt Disney made a short cartoon in 1922 simply called Cinderella.

237. Cinderella's shoe size is 4½.

238. Although Cinderella is one of the most famous fictional princesses ever, she was heavily criticised at the time for being one-dimensional, boring, and passive. Some critics even accused her of being a gold-digger.

239. Disney decided to remake all of their classic animated films into live action. The 2015 remake, Cinderella, was the first movie to get this treatment.

240. Walt Disney said that the transformation of Cinderella's dress was the greatest thing his team had ever animated.

Cloudy with a Chance of Meatballs
2009

241. Mr T. voices Earl Devereaux. Earl's hairstyle is the exact opposite of Mr. T's. Mr. T has a T-shaped hairstyle. Earl has a T-shaped bald patch.

242. The tagline is, "Prepare to get served."

243. Bill Hader voices Flint. His lab is based on Nikola Tesla's laboratory.

244. In Israel, the film is called It's Raining Falafel.

245. Anna Faris voices Sam Sparks. Amy Poehler nearly voiced the character.

246. Bruce Campbell voices Mayor Shelbourne. He never met Bill Hader until after the production ended since they recorded their lines separately.

247. The story is based on the 1978 novel of the same name.

248. The film had a sequel which revolved around living food called foodimals. The writers came up with 120 puns for the foodimals including Tacodile, Sasquash, Fruit Cockatiel, Shrimpanzee, Flamango, Susheep, Wildebeet, Watermelphant, Lemmongs, and Buffaloaf. Only 39 were used for the final cut.

Coco
2017

249. John Ratzenberger cameos in almost every Pixar film. In Coco, he provides the voice of Juan Ortodoncia. He is the skeleton who can cross over to The Land of the Living because his dentist remembers him.

250. The hardest thing to animate was Abuelita's neck.

251. The film won an Oscar for Best Animated Feature. Remember Me won for the Oscar for Best Original Song.

252. In The Land of the Dead, the colourful houses are stacked on top of each other. This is inspired by the buildings in the Mexican city of Guanajuato.

253. The film made $150 million in five days. It made more in 19 days than Cars 3 did in over five months. It went on to make $806 million at the box office. Coco was #1 at the box office for three weeks in the US. It spent more time at #1 at the box office than any animated film in the 21st century.

    Unsurprisingly, it went on to become the most successful film in Mexican history.

254. The heavy metal band is called Escapula, which means "Shoulder Blade."

255. This is the ninth Pixar film to win an Oscar for Best Animated Feature. It is the third Pixar film to win an Oscar for Best Original Song.

256. Benjamin Bratt voices Ernesto. This is the fourth animated film he has starred in since he appeared in Despicable Me 2 and Cloudy with a Chance of Meatballs 1 and 2.

257. China have incredibly strict censors and rarely allow a film to be shown in their country if death plays a major theme. The Chinese censor board were so touched by this film's message, they allowed it to be released.

258. During the credits, a picture of over a hundred deceased people who inspired the filmmakers appears. Walt Disney's photo is in the middle.

The Croods
2013

259.   Nicholas Cage was offered the titular role in Shrek but he turned it down. He said it was the biggest regret of his career and he shouldn't have underestimated an animated film. When he was offered the Grug in this film, he accepted.

260.   The original title was Crood's Awakening.

261.   The story was supposed to be a buddy comedy between Guy and Grug.

262.   The film stars many actors who have appeared in Marvel movies including Nicholas Cage (Ghost Rider,) Emma Stone, (Gwen Stacy in Amazing Spider-Man,) and Ryan Reynolds (Deadpool.)

263.   Almost none of the animals in the film ever existed. Most of the creatures are chimaeras; a fusion of multiple animals put together.

264.   It took eight years to make the film.

265.   The tagline is "Meet the first modern family."

266.   The Croods have no idea what the outside world is like because Grug won't let them leave the cave.
    This idea is based on a concept called Plato's Cave. The Greek philosopher, Plato, described a scenario where a group of people are chained to a cave wall. There is a fire behind them which projects shadows onto the wall in front of the chained men. If something passes the fire e.g. a fly, a bird, a rat, etc. its shadow will be projected on the wall.

Since this is all the men can see, this is the only reality the men are aware of. Because of this, the men would have no desire to leave the cave because they are unaware of a world beyond it.

Ferdinand
2017

267. The film is based on The Story of Ferdinand, which was written by Munro Leaf in 1936. During World War II, it was banned in Italy, Germany and Russia for being "too nice."

268. Una, Dos, and Quatro's spinning motion is based on Sonic the Hedgehog's spinball attack in the Sonic video game series.

269. John Cena voices Ferdinand. This is the fourth animated film he has worked on.

270. Kate McKinnon voices Lupe. This is the third animated film she has worked on since she starred in The Angry Birds Movie and Finding Dory.

271. Ferdinand lives in Ronda in the south of Spain. This village has the world's oldest bull-ring. It was built in 1785.

272. This is the fourth film that Blue Sky Studios have made that is based on a book. The other films were Horton Hears a Who!, Epic, and The Peanuts Movie.

273. The film spawned a mobile game called Ferdinand: Unstoppabull.

274. The film was meant to be released in July 2017 but it was delayed so it wouldn't have to compete with summer blockbusters. Ironically, it came out the same day as Star Wars: The Last Jedi.

275. At one point, Angus says, "I'm a bull, not a doctor." It refers to the famous line, "I'm a doctor, not a

mechanic," that Dr Bones McCoy says throughout Star Trek.

276. This is the sixth animated film that Carolos Saldanha has directed. He directed Ice Age, Ice Age 2, Ice Age 3, Rio, Rio 2, and Robots.

277. Disney made a short called Ferdinand the Bull in 1938.

Ferngully:
The Last Rainforest
1992

278. This was the first animated film that Robin Williams starred in. He voices Batty Koda.

279. The tagline was, "Do you believe in humans?"

280. Ferngully is based on the rainforest of Australia.

281. The film was directed by Bill Kroyer. This is the only film he ever made.

282. Elton John performed the song, Some Other World. It was the first time he worked on an animated film.

283. Many people complain that the film, Avatar, copied the story of Ferngully.

284. The film's message is to protect the rainforest. Many critics pointed out the irony of making an animated film with this message since thousands of trees had to be cut down to make the paper for the animation.

Final Fantasy VII: Advent Children
2005

285. Mena Suvari voices Aerith. She is best-known for playing Angela in American Beauty and Heather in American Pie.

286. Cloud uses five Limit Breaks in the film.

287. The final battle had to be re-animated as it was considered too gory.

288. Loz's ring tone is the Final Fantasy Victory music.

289. When Loz fights Tifa, the background music is the Battle theme from the video game series.

290. In the original trailer, all the characters looked Asian. In this film, all the characters look more anime-like.

291. The tagline is "I won't just be a memory."

292. Kadaj calls upon the dragon, Bahamut. In Final Fantasy VII, there are three versions of this dragon; Bahamut, Neo Bahamut, and Bahamut Zero. The dragon in the film is called Bahamut Sin.

293. Vincent's three-barrelled gun is called Cerberus. It is named after the three-headed dog that guards the gates of Tartarus in Greek mythology.

294. Cloud's bike is called Fenrir. It is named after a monstrous wolf in Norse mythology.

Final Fantasy:
The Spirits Within
2001

295. There's an extra on the DVD that shows the main characters performing Michael Jackson's thriller.

296. Ming-Na Wen voices the lead character, Aki. She also voices the titular character in the Disney film, Mulan.

297. Donald Sutherland voices Sid. There's a character called Sid in almost every Final Fantasy game.

298. The film cost $137 million. It only made $85 million at the box office, making it one of the most unsuccessful films ever at the time.
    Despite the fact the film was a flop, it had the highest rating of any movie based on a video game according to Rotten Tomatoes at the time.

299. The story takes place in 2065.

300. Although most characters and objects were computer-generated, the backgrounds were hand painted.

301. The film took four years to make. As the animators were finishing the last few shots, they had to fix some of the earliest shots because they looked so dated by comparison.

302. The animators spent 20% of their time making sure Aki's hair looked right.

303. Ving Rhames voices Ryan. Originally, Ryan was going to have a cybernetic arm. This is a reference to Barrett from Final Fantasy VII who had a robotic arm.

304. Matt McKenzie voices the Major. He voices Auron in Final Fantasy X. He is the only actor to voice a character in this film and the video game series.

Finding Nemo
2003

305. Dory is a Regal Blue Tang fish. Marlin is a clownfish. The success of this film led to Tang fish and clownfish becoming popular pets.

    Sadly, both fish are very difficult to look after and many pet owners accidentally killed them. Some pet owners took the "setting fish free" concept too literally. Many children chucked their fish down the toilet, believing it would lead them to the sea. These fish died before they reached the sewer.

    Some pet owners bought clownfish just so they could release them in the sea, not knowing that the species is venomous, which decimated the ecology in certain areas, especially in Florida.

    Also, the demand for clownfish was so high, the fisherman struggled to find them. In certain areas, the clownfish population dropped by 75%.

306. It took the animators four days to work on one frame of the underwater scenes. One frame of footage makes up $1/24^{th}$ of a second.

307. The animators studied how light passes through gummy bears to understand how light passes through fish.

308. At the end of the film, the fish escape from a net by swimming downward, breaking free from the attached ship.

    The weirdest thing about this scene is that it is based on a real incident. In Norway, a group of fish capsized a ship by swimming down while trapped in the ship's net.

309. Nemo plans to escape from a fish tank by damaging the filter. The filmmakers' dismantled the biofiltration unit of a fish tank to make sure this concept was plausible.

310. Dory's short-term memory loss is a reference to the misconception that goldfish have a three-second memory. In reality, goldfish can remember things for up to a month.

311. Originally, the audience wouldn't know why Marlin was so protective of Nemo for most the movie. This was changed as it made Marlin come across as annoying and unsympathetic.

312. Willem Dafoe voices Gill. The scars on Gill's face is based on the creases on Dafoe's face.

313. Gill was originally going to be Marlin's sidekick instead of Dory.

314. Although Marlin's species is often known as a clownfish, its biological name is an anemonefish.

315. In real life, clownfish are hermaphrodites.

316. The boats at the dock are called Major Plot Point, For the Birds, Skiff-A-Dee-Do-Dah, Sea Monkey, Peer Pressure, Bow Movement, Knottie Buoy, The Surly Mermaid, and iBoat.

317. The film cost $94 million. It grossed $940 million at the box office, making it the first animated film to be more successful than The Lion King. When the producer of The Lion King heard this, he said, "It's about time."

318. Gill's eclectic group in the fish tank are based on the characters in the film, One Flew Over the Cuckoo's Nest.

319. Nemo's name is a reference to Captain Nemo in Jules Verne's novel, 20,000 Leagues Under the Sea. It means "nobody" in Latin.

320. There was supposed to be a scene where the sharks are playing volleyball with sea mines.

321. The seagulls are modelled after the penguin from the Wallace and Gromit short, The Wrong Trousers.

322. The tagline is, "71% of the Earth's surface is covered by water. That's a lot of space to find one fish."

323. This is the first Pixar film that doesn't take place in the United States.

324. The director, Andrew Stanton, pitched the idea to Pixar in an hour-long presentation. When he finished, the head of Pixar said, "You had me at fish."

Flushed Away
2006

325. The film was made by Aardman studios; the same studio that makes the Wallace and Gromit animations.

326. This was the first CGI-film that Aardman made.

327. In one scene, Hugh Jackman's character, Roddy, pulls out a Wolverine outfit from a wardrobe. Hugh Jackman portrays Wolverine in the X-Men films.

328. At the start of the film, one of the outfits that Roddy pulls out of the wardrobe belongs to Wallace from Wallace and Gromit.

329. Kate Winslet voices Rita. Nicole Kidman was considered for the role.

330. One of the frozen rats in the fridge is Han Solo from Star Wars.

331. Jean Reno voices Le Frog. Johnny Depp and Kevin Kline were considered for the role.

332. A picture of Shrek appears on the fridge.

333. The tagline is "Plumbing soon."

334. When Roddy gets flushed, an orange fish shouts, "Have you seen my dad?" This is a reference to Finding Nemo.

335. The Toad wears a Freemason ring.

336. Andy Serkis voices Spike. Robert De Niro auditioned for the role.

Foodfight!
2012

337. This is considered to be the worst 3D animated film ever.

338. The story revolves around food products coming to life when there are no humans around. (Basically, it's Toy Story with food.)
    Many food brands were supposed to appear like Count Chocula and Chester Cheetah but they pulled out, believing the film would fail at the box office.

339. The film was directed by Lawrence Kasanoff. He tried to make a Tetris film but his story was so complex, he believed it could only work as a trilogy. He is still working on it.

340. The director was certain this film would be a hit and claimed his company was "the new Pixar." The film cost $65 million. It only made $73,706 at the box office. This means that it made slightly more than 0.1% of its budget back.

341. If the film was successful, the director was going to create an event called Foodfight on Ice, similar to Disney on Ice.

342. The film was supposed to come out in 2003. It was delayed for nine years. The reason why Foodfight! was so heavily delayed is because the hard drive containing key footage was stolen. This means that the animators lost years of work and had to start all over again.

343. According to the animators, the director didn't understand the difference between live-action and animation. He asked the crew to do "retakes" of the

scenes and told the animators to make the scenes "more awesome" and "30% better." The director was fired due to his incompetence and the studio had to finish the remainder of the film.

344. Many animators who worked on the film don't mention it on their resumes.

The Fox and the Hound
1981

345. The fox is called Tod. Tod is derived from the Middle English word "todde" which means "fox."

346. The tagline is "Two friends that didn't know they were supposed to be enemies."

347. The film was delayed for a year as many animators left to join Disney's competitor, Don Bluth.

348. The story is based on Daniel P. Mannix's novel of the same. The film has very little resemblance to the novel.

349. Kurt Russell voices Copper. Corey Feldman voices Young Copper.

350. Renowned director, Tim Burton, animated the character, Vixey.

351. Mickey Rooney voices Tod.

352. The sequel, The Fox and the Hound 2, was released in 2006.

353. The bear's roar is the same as Shere Kahn's roar in The Jungle Book.

Frankenweenie
2012

354. If the film wasn't allowed to be in black-and-white, Tim Burton wouldn't have made it.

355. Zero's grave can be seen in the pet cemetery. Zero was the name of the dog in The Nightmare Before Christmas.

356. Shelley the tortoise becomes a gigantic monster. This is a reference to the film, Gamera, which revolves around a colossal tortoise-like creature.

357. One of the graves in the pet cemetery reads "Goodbye Kitty." It resembles the Hello Kitty logo.

358. Burton made the 1984 version of Frankenweenie when he worked for Disney. Disney considered the film to be too scary for children and had Burton fired.

359. Elsa's dog is called Persephone. Persephone was the wife of Hades in Greek mythology.

360. Persephone has a white streak in her hair, just like the Bride in Bride of Frankenstein.

Frozen
2013

361. The film won two Oscars, two BAFTAs, and a Golden Globe.

362. Elsa's original look was based on Amy Winehouse.

363. In most films, good characters wear bright colours and villains wear dark colours. In this film, the villain wears the brightest clothing.

364. In 2013, an animated film called The Legend of Sarila was released. The creators changed the title to Frozen Land when it was released in the US to capitalise on the success of Frozen. Even the font of the title was the same as Frozen and the main character was wearing the same colours as Anna.

    The filmmakers hoped consumers would think the movie was connected to Frozen even though the story revolves around Eskimos and shamans.

    Weirdly, Oscar-winning actor, Christopher Plummer, starred in this film.

365. Walt Disney wanted to make this film in the 1940s.

366. Ciaran Hinds voices Pabbie and Grandpa.

367. Two of the guards are called Kai and Gerda. This is the name of two characters in the original story, The Snow Queen.

368. The movie is 102 minutes long. Only 24 minutes is dedicated to the songs.

369. Santino Fontana voices Hans. He originally auditioned for Kristoff.

370. Santino Fontana sang I Feel Pretty for his audition.

371. The giant snowman is called Marshmallow.

372. Marshmallow was originally going to look like a gigantic version of Olaf.

373. When Marshmallow throws Anna, she loses her hat. She has her hat back in the next scene.

374. The movie was supposed to be in 2D.

375. 312 different faces were created for the characters in this film, which was more than any other animated Disney film at the time.

376. The most complex frames in the movie were when Elsa walks onto the balcony of her castle. It took 132 hours to render each frame.

377. Let It Go was written in one day by Robert Lopez. Lopez has also written music for the musicals, The Book of Mormon and Avenue Q.

378. In this film, there is no explanation why Elsa can create ice. In the original script, one child is born with ice powers every millennium when the planets align with Saturn.

379. The film spawned a short called Frozen Fever in 2015. It took six months to make this short.

380. When Elsa sneezes in Frozen Fever, she creates mini-snowman called Snowgies. Baymax from Big Hero 6 cameos as one of the Snowgies.

381. In the original script of Frozen Fever, Elsa created Olafs every time she sneezed. The writers decided not to do this as they didn't want to oversaturate the character.

382. There is an Internet rumour that Elsa's parents didn't die at sea. Instead, they were washed up in Africa and were killed by a wild animal and their child grew up to be Tarzan.

Fun & Fancy Free
1947

383. This was the first film that Mickey Mouse appeared in since Fantasia.

384. A portion of the film revolves around the Jack and the Beanstalk story. Billy Gilbert voices Willie the Giant. Gilbert also voices Sneezy in Snow White and the Seven Dwarfs.

385. This was the first film to credit the voice actor for Mickey Mouse. He was voiced by some guy called Walt Disney.

386. It took seven years to complete the film. The reason why it took so long was because the American military forced Disney's studio to make propaganda shorts after the US entered World War II. In 1942, 90% of Walt Disney's 550 employees were making war-based films.

387. Although Mickey Mouse was the most popular animated character during the 1930s, he was overshadowed in the 1940s by Donald Duck and Goofy. The story of Mickey and the Beanstalk was inserted into this movie to help Mickey Mouse regain his popularity.

388. Mickey and the Beanstalk was originally called The Legend of Happy Valley.

389. This was the first time where Mickey, Donald, and Goofy starred in a cartoon since The Whalers in 1938.

390. This was the last time that Walt Disney voiced Mickey Mouse in an animated feature.

Ghost in the Shell
1995

391. This was the first anime ever funded by the UK, the US, and Japan. It was also the first anime to be released in the US, the UK, and Japan simultaneously.

392. The song in the credits was played by U2.

393. The Japanese title is Mobile-Armoured Riot Police.

394. The film cost $10 million. It only made $515,905 at the box office.

395. Steven Spielberg said this movie has one of the best stories ever. He incorporated the idea of a robot having a soul for his 2001 film, AI.

396. Scarlet Johansson plays the main character in the live-action 2017 film, Ghost in the Shell. The role nearly went to Margot Robbie.

397. Although Motoko looks like a woman, she acts gender-neutral.

398. The sequel, Ghost in the Shell: Innocence, was released in 2004.

399. The film spawned an animated series called Ghost in the Shell: Stand Alone Complex in 2002. This show spawned a film called Solid State Society in 2006.

400. Although the film is Japanese, it was more successful in the Western world than in Japan. The director believes the film didn't do well in Japan because the Internet plays a huge part in the film, which was an alien concept in Japan at the time.

Hercules
2000

401. When Hercules becomes well-known, he starts endorsing products and making appearances for money. Although this seems over-the-top, this was exactly what Ancient Greek athletes used to do.

402. David Bowie and Willem Dafoe were considered for Hades. The studio offered Jack Nicholson $500,00 to voice Hades. Nicholson said he would only voice the role for $15 million and 50% of all Hades merchandise. The studio refused.

    John Lithgow was cast as Hades and recorded all his dialogue but he was replaced by James Woods.

403. Rip Torn voices Zeus. John Goodman was considered for the role.

404. In Greek myth, the god of the dead is Pluto. Hades is the Roman god of the dead. In Greek myth, Pluto is not evil. His brothers, Zeus and Poseidon, committed far more evil acts.

405. In the film, the Titans were banished by Zeus. In Greek myth, Zeus' grandfather, Uranus sealed away the Titans. The leader of the Titans was Zeus' father, Cronus.

406. When Phil meets Hercules, he said, "Two words: I am retired." In Greek, "I am retired." translates as "Eimai syntaxiochos.," which is two words.

407. Hades' minions are called Pain and Panic. Their names are translated from Phobos and Deimos. Phobos and Deimos were minions of the Greek god of war, Ares.

408. When Hades is eating worms, the voice-actor, James Woods, was eating a watermelon.

409. Contrary to popular believe, Hercules is based on a Roman demi-god. His Greek name is Herakles.

410. In Greek myth, Herakles killed his wife, Megara, after Zeus' wife, Hera, drove him insane.

Howl's Moving Castle
2004

411. When Christian Bale saw Hayao Miyazaki's film, Spirited Away, he told Miyazaki that he would play any part in his next film. Miyazaki cast him as the titular character, Howl, in this film.

412. The film is based on the book of the same name. It was written by Diana Wynne Jones in 1986. Jones wrote another book called Castle in the Sky, which was also adapted into a film by Hayao Miyazaki.

413. War plays a heavy theme in the film. Weirdly, war isn't referenced in the novel.

414. Legendary actress, Lauren Bacall, voices the Witch of the Waste.

415. At one point, Markl gorges on food. Miyazaki incorporates gorging in most of his films.

416. Billy Crystal voices Calcifer.

417. Although it's not clear in the film, Sophie is a witch.

The Incredibles
2004

418. The baby is called Jack-Jack. This is the nickname of the director's son.

419. The scene where Frozone gets a drink while at gunpoint was inspired by a scene where Samuel L. Jackson's character in Die Hard with a Vengeance is on the phone while being held at gun point.

420. Upon its release, The Incredibles was the only Pixar film to win two Oscars.

421. Mirage's phone number spells out "SUPERHERO."

422. Mr. Incredible works for Insuracare. In the Singapore version of the film, the company is called Black Hearted Insurance Company.

423. The superheroes on Syndrome's database include Stormicide, Tradewind, Blitzerman, Apogee, Vectress, Blazestone, Macroburst, Psycwave, Everseer, Phylange, Downburst, Hyper Shock, and Gamma Jack.

424. The animators believed this film couldn't be made any sooner since the technology wasn't good enough to render human beings realistically.

425. When Brad Bird first approached Pixar to greenlight the film, he was told that it would take ten years to make and would cost a fortune. In the end, the film only cost $92 million. It made $633 million at the box office.

426. The DVD came with a short called Jack-Jack Attack.

427. The action figure of Elastigirl is called Mrs. Incredible because DC Comics owns the copyrights for the name "Elastigirl."

428. The Incredibles live in Metroville. The city is named after Superman's homes; Smallville and Metropolis.

429. All extra characters (the other superheroes, the children, the henchmen) have the same design. It is called the Universal Model.

430. Spencer Fox voices Dash. He ran around the studio before he had to record scenes where Dash was exhausted.

431. Jack-Jack is the only member of the Incredibles' family that makes physical contact with Syndrome.

432. Wallace Shawn voices Bob's boss, Gilbert Huph. Shawn voices Rex in the Toy Story movies.

433. Huph's pencils read "Your Life Is In Our Hands."

434. Dash can run 200mph.

435. This is the first Pixar film where the Pizza Express truck from Toy Story doesn't cameo.

436. Syndrome's computer is based on Cerebro from the X-Men comics.

437. Brad Bird believes that most superhero movies start with an action scene before the audience has a chance to know the characters. To focus on the characters, Brad decided to begin the film with the superheroes being interviewed.

438. The DVD has a terrible cartoon that shows the adventures of Mr. Incredible and Frozone. The cartoon also has an audio commentary with the two characters. Most of the commentary involves Frozone complaining that the cartoon changed his skin tone. He says things like, "I'm white? They made me a white guy?!" Mr. Incredible tries to calm him down by saying, "Well... maybe the prints faded."

439. There was a petition to get Barack Obama and Michelle Obama to act out the "Where's My Super Suit?" scene.

Inside Out
2015

440. Kaitlyn Dias voices Riley. She was never supposed to play the character. Originally, it was her job to read the storyboard narration. The animators got use to her voice and asked her to voice the lead role.

441. The noises that Riley makes as a baby are taken directly from Boo in the film, Monsters, Inc.

442. Riley's father daydreams about football. In some countries, this daydream was changed to ice hockey.

443. Nemo appears on a board game called Find Me when Joy and Sadness are in Imagination Land.

444. Despite the film's complexity, it was made by 45 animators. That's half the animators that Pixar had on their other films.

445. Riley's chief emotion is Joy. Her mother's is Sadness and her father's is Anger.

446. The film cost $175 million. It made $857 million at the box office.

447. In France, the film is called Vice-Versa.

448. The newspaper that Anger reads is called The Mind Reader. The articles he reads always relate to what's happening to Riley.

449. Some of the memory balls in Riley's minds contain scenes from other Pixar films.

450. Between 2005-2009, Denise Daniels repeatedly pitched Disney an animated show called The Moodsters. It revolved around characters "representing a single emotion with a corresponding colour."

In 2017, she took Pixar to court as she believes Inside Out is a rip-off of her pitched show.

The Iron Giant
1999

451. The film was nearly made in 1991 by Don Bluth. Bluth is known for making The Land Before Time, An American Tail, and All Dogs Go To Heaven.

452. The Iron Giant had higher ratings than any film distributed by Warner Brothers in 15 years.

453. Although it cost $70 million, it only made $31 million back.

454. Brad Bird saw audience members wincing at the scene where Hogarth whacks his face into a branch. He said he was proud of this as he finds it very difficult to display pain in a 2D cartoon.

455. Ted Hughes wrote the original story to comfort his children after they lost their mother, Sylvia Plath.

456. Although the film is drastically different to the original novel, Ted Hughes was very happy with the story that Brad Bird created. Sadly, he never saw the film as he died one year before the film premiered.

457. The original novel's official title is The Iron Man: A Children's Story in Five Nights. It was published in 1968 and is only 59 pages long.

458. The novel revolves around The Iron Man protecting the world from a continent-sized alien called The Space-Bat-Angel-Demon.

459. The Iron Man novel spawned a sequel in 1993 called The Iron Woman. In this book, the Iron Woman punishes humanity for polluting the world.

460. The film nearly concluded with the caption, "THE END...or is it?"

461. The tagline is "Some secrets are too huge to hide."

462. Although the film is 2D, the Giant is 3D. The director made this decision to make the Giant not fit with the other characters since he is an alien.

463. SPOILER – At the beginning of the film, the Soviet satellite, Sputnik, makes a beeping sound. During this time, the United States had a hostile relationship with Russia and were worried they could be attacked or invaded at any moment.

   At the end of the film, a beeping sound can be heard. It is revealed that this beeping sound is a homing signal so the Iron Giant can reassemble his body. This is supposed to represent that people fear the unknown. People feared the Iron Giant and Sputnik because humanity didn't understand what their purpose was.

   However, if people tried to understand the Giant, they would've learned that he wasn't a threat. If Americans tried to communicate with Russia during the 1950s, there would've been a lot less paranoia.

   The audience was supposed understand all of this from a beep.

The Jungle Book
1967

464. Sterling Holloway voices Kaa. Holloway also voices the Cheshire Cat in Alice in Wonderland.

465. The sequel, The Jungle Book 2, was released in 2003. Haley Joel Osment voices Mowgli, John Goodman voices Baloo, and Tony Jay voices Shere Kahn.

466. A short-sighted rhino called Rocky was cut from the film at the last minute.

467. The film was directed by Wolfgang Reitherman. He directed many Disney films including 101 Dalmatians, Robin Hood, The Sword in the Stone, The AristoCats, and The Rescuers.

468. Despite what many people believe, black panthers like Bagheera don't exist. Any animal that was mistaken as a black panther was actually a black leopard. If you look at a black leopard closely, you can see it has spots.

469. This is the most successful film in German history.

470. The vulture song, That's What Friends Are For, was supposed to be a rock song.

471. Kaa's name is supposed to be pronounced "Kahr" according to the writer.

472. The only song that was in the original script that made it into the final cut was The Bare Necessities. The song won an Oscar.

473. In the book, Mowgli is the only one who can resist Kaa's hypnotic stare.

474. George Sanders voices Shere Kahn. He is the first Oscar-winning actor to have a role in an animated Disney film.

475. In the novel, Shere Kahn has a sidekick called Tabaqui the Cowardly Jackal.

476. This is one of the most successful films in the history of the UK.

477. Bruce Reitherman performed the voice of Mowgli. He is the son of the director. Nowadays, he makes documentaries about wild life.

478. Most people mispronounce Mowgli's name. It's pronounced "MAU-glee." This was confirmed by the writer's daughter, Elsie. She never forgave Disney for this mistake.

Klaus
2019

479. Despite how the animation appears, the film is 2D, not 3D.

480. The town of Smeerensburg is based on a real town in Norway called Smeerenburg. It was a prominent location for whaling during the 17th century.

481. Many studios turned down the film because it was "too risky."

482. JK Simmons voices the Drill Sergeant and Klaus AKA Santa. Simmons used to work as a mall Santa.

483. The film cost $40 million.

484. The tagline is, "Welcome to the jingle."

485. The residents and buildings of Smeerensburg were designed with sharp angles and triangles to come across as unfriendly. This is a common technique in animation and was used for the dogs in Up and for the character of Jafar in Aladdin.

486. Jesper was meant to be a chimney sweep.

487. Jesper's name means "treasure."

Kubo and the Two Strings
2016

488. The Moon Beast is the first character in a stop-motion film that was entirely created from a 3D printer.

489. The tagline is "Be bold. Be brave. Be epic."

490. Art Parkin plays Kubo. He is from Donegal in Ireland. Since he was in his home country at the time of the audition, he read for the role through his mother's iPad and then sent it to the casting director.

491. Matthew McConaughey voices Beetle. His character speaks in a neutral voice. McConaughey found this extremely difficult due to his thick Texan accent.

492. McConaughey did push-ups before recording any intense scenes.

493. The giant skeleton is the biggest stop-motion puppet in movie history, standing 16ft.

494. Although the film was highly praised, it didn't do well at the box office as it only made $70 million. Since it cost $60 million, it only made a measly $10 million profit.

495. The word, "story," is uttered 31 times. It is said 13 times in the last 15 minutes.

496. When Art Parkinson was cast as Kubo, the director was disappointed to learn his voice had gotten deeper since he went through puberty. Since Art just finished working with Dwayne "The Rock" Johnson in the film, San Andreas, the director joked that hanging around Johnson made Art hit puberty at super-speed.

Kung Fu Panda
2008

497. The animators took a six-hour kung fu class to get an idea of how the martial arts should be portrayed. They also spent years studying Chinese art and watching tons of kung fu movies.

498. Po's fighting style is Bear.

499. Chinese film distributors said the film depicts ancient China more accurately than most Chinese films.

500. The markings on Viper's back are Chinese poetry.

501. Every time an animator finished a scene, they were rewarded with a fortune cookie.

502. Kai appears in Po's dream in the beginning. Kai is the main villain in Kung Fu Panda 3.

503. Angelina Jolie voices Tigress. Jolie has a tiger tattoo on her back.

504. Tigress' markings are designed to resemble make-up.

505. Chop Kick Panda is a 2011 rip-off of Kung Fu Panda. The whole film was made with Flash animation.

The Lego Movie
2014

506. It was extremely difficult to secure the rights to use Superman in this film.

507. Batman's license plate is BAT2DBONE.

508. Originally, Metalbeard was going to be Emmet's partner, not Batman.

509. The film cost $60 million. At the time of its release, The Lego Movie was the most successful animated film released by Warner Bros, making $460 million.

510. Cobie Smulders voices Wonder Woman. She was in the running to play the same character in the film, Wonder Woman.

511. Channing Tatum voices Superman. Jonah Hill voices Green Lantern. Nick Offerman voices Metalbeard. All these actors starred in 21 Jump Street.

512. Charlie Day voices Benny the 1980-Something Space Guy. His helmet is cracked and worn-out. This is a reference to the fact that this Lego figure was criticized because it's helmet easily cracked.

513. Liam Neeson wasn't available at the same time as Will Ferrell so they recorded their scene on the phone.

514. The scriptwriters intended there to be a song called Everything is Awesome before the lyrics were written. They wanted the song to be the most annoyingly catchy song possible.

515. Lord Business was to be called Black Falcon.

516. When Emmet flies through the air after the Wild West scene, you can see a pig in the background. When the pig hits the ground, it explodes into sausages.

517. In an early script, R2-D2 and Indiana Jones were main characters.

518. Lego sales boosted by 15% shortly after the film was released.

519. Will Forte voices Abraham Lincoln. He is incorrectly called "Orville Forte" in the credits.

520. This is the first film to feature Wonder Woman.

521. The credits were done with stop-motion. It took over a year to complete the animation.

522. C-3PO and Lando Carissian are voiced by the actors who portrayed them in the Star Wars films.

523. When Wyldstyle flips a table in the Melting Room, a schedule can be seen on the bottom that reads, "DON'T FORGET TO CLEAN THE LASER!!" This is followed by another note that reads, "HOW ABOUT YOU CLEAN IT."

524. There was going to be a scene where every character that Johnny Depp has ever played would meet up and talk to each other.

The Lion King
1994

525. Although Rafiki is supposed to be a mandrill, he has a tail, which mandrills lack.

526. When Mufasa and Simba talk about the stars, the constellation for Leo is clearly visible. Leo represents the lion.

527. Simba's mother, Sarabi, was supposed to sing a song called The Lion in the Moon but it was cut.

528. Hakuna Matata wasn't in the original script.

529. The stampede was so difficult to animate, the creators had to write a new program to control the wildebeests' movements.

530. The film won two Oscars. Elton John won an Oscar for Best Original Song and Hans Zimmer won for Best Original Score.

531. There were 15 different versions of Can You Feel the Love Tonight?

532. The film inspired the Broadway musical which opened in 1997. It won six Tony Awards, including Best Musical.

533. None of the lion roars were from actual lions. Frank Welker provided all the lion roars himself by screaming into a trash can.

534. An earthquake occurred near Walt Disney Studios in 1994 which forced the animators to complete their drawings at home.

535. In 1994, Disney made over a billion dollars from Lion King merchandise.

536. Simba's mane was inspired by Jon Bon Jovi's hair.

537. The film inspired a sequel in 1998 called The Lion King 2: Simba's Pride. Since The Lion King is based on Hamlet, the creators of the sequel decided to maintain the Shakespeare motif and based the sequel's story on Romeo and Juliet.

538. The film inspired a sequel/prequel/sidequel called The Lion King 1½ which revolves around Timon and Pumbaa before, during, and after the events in The Lion King. It is based on the play, Rosencrantz and Guildenstern Are Dead.

539. The film inspired an animated series called Timon & Pumbaa which ran for five seasons.

540. The gopher was supposed to be a naked mole rat but the artists couldn't draw it properly.

541. According to the director, this film takes place before humanity existed.

542. During the song, Be Prepared, Jeremy Irons roars, "You won't get a sniff without me!" He strained his throat so much when he said that line that he lost his voice and couldn't continue the song. The rest of the song is voiced by Jim Cummings who sings in Jeremy Irons voice perfectly. The transition is so seamless, it's impossible to notice.

The Little Mermaid
1989

543. The shark is called Glut.

544. Ariel and Sebastian are named after two characters from William Shakespeare's The Tempest.

545. This was the first Disney film to win an Oscar since Bedknobs and Broomsticks in 1971.

546. There is a rumour that Prince Eric is related to Prince Philip from Sleeping Beauty.

547. In one draft, Ursula was Triton's sister.

548. Despite what many people believe, Sebastian doesn't speak with a Jamaican accent. Sebastian has a Trinidadian (or Trini) accent.

549. Originally, Sebastian was going to be British.

550. Ursula is based on the drag performer, Divine.

551. Ursula's gestures are based on the villain from The Rescuers, Madame Medusa.

552. Flounder's fish species doesn't exist.

553. The film spawned a sequel in 2000 called The Little Mermaid 2: Return to the Sea. The story revolves around Ariel's daughter and Ursula's evil sister, Morgana.

554. Mickey Mouse's head can be seen in Ursula's contract.

555. The film had a prequel in 2008 called The Little Mermaid: Ariel's Beginning.

556. The final scene took a year to animate. It was so difficult to draw, the animators had to rewatch the ocean scenes in Pinocchio to make the water's movements look right.

557. This was the first successful animated Disney film in decades. This began what is often known as the Disney Renaissance Era.

558. According to the producer, the final scene was inspired by Die Hard. I swear that's true.

559. The original fairy-tale is very different from the movie. In Hans Christian Anderson's version, the Mermaid (who has no name) makes a deal with a sea witch so she can walk on land. The sea witch agrees to this deal but only after cutting off the mermaid's tongue. The witch also states that the Mermaid will turn into foam if the one she loves decides to marry anyone but her.

Although the Mermaid is granted legs, it feels like she is walking on knives. Although the prince falls for her, he decides to marry someone else.

The Mermaid's sister tells her that she will return to being a Mermaid if she kills the prince with an enchanted blade. The Mermaid says she can't kill the one she loves and thus, jumps into the ocean, bursting into foam.

The Spirits of the Air are won over by her sacrifice and give her a soul so she can ascend to the afterlife…but only after she commits three centuries of good deeds. (Weirdly, doing tests for 300 years is a common theme in European folklore.)

The Lorax
2012

560. Danny DeVito voices the titular character. He also voices the character in German, Russian, Italian, and Spanish.

561. The story is based on Dr. Seuss' book of the same name. The 45-page book was published in 1971.

562. Zac Efron voices Ted. Ted is named after the original author. Dr. Seuss' real name was Theodore "Ted" Geisel.

563. Taylor Swift voices Audrey.

564. The film was released on Dr. Seuss' birthday, March 2nd.

565. The movie was criticized for warning children about corporate greed and yet it contained over 70 advertised products.

The Lord of the Rings
1978

566. This story focuses on the first two-thirds of the original novel. This film was supposed to have a sequel that covered the final third of the story. Sadly, the film bombed at the box office and the sequel was scrapped.

567. John Hurt voices Aragorn.

568. The film used an animation style called rotoscope. This required the crew to film actors in black-and-white and draw an animation cell over every frame.

569. The film was supposed to have Led Zeppelin songs but the director couldn't get the music rights.

570. The two main villains are Sauron and Saruman. The producers worried that the characters' names sounded too similar so they changed Saruman's name to "Aruman." Although this decision was reversed, Saruman is still referred to as "Aruman" several times.

571. Anthony Daniels voiced Legolas. Daniels is best-known for playing C-3P0 in the Star Wars films.

572. The director of the live-action Lord of the Rings, Peter Jackson, copied certain shots including when the Ringwraiths slash the beds to ribbons.

573. The actors who voiced Frodo and Perry are brothers.

574. Orson Welles narrated the trailer.

575. Visionary director, Tim Burton, was one of the animators. It was his first job on a film.

Mary and Max
2009

576. One of the tombstones in the graveyard reads, "RIP Adam Elliot. Very over-rated. Elliott is the director."

577. This was the only film that Adam Elliot directed.

578. The story revolves around a girl called Mary who becomes pen pals with an autistic man called Max. According to the director, Max is based on "a pen-friend in New York who I've been writing to for over 20 years."

579. It took nine weeks to design and build the set.

580. It took over a year just to do principal photography for the film.

581. 133 mini-sets, 212 puppets, and 475 props were made for the film.

Meet the Robinsons
2007

582. The story is based on the book, A Day with Wilbur Robinson.

583. The film was originally going to be live-action.

584. Jim Carrey was offered two roles but he turned them down to star in The Number 23.

585. Adam West voices Uncle Art.

586. There is a picture of Nikola Tesla in Lewis' wall in the orphanage.

587. The test-screening went so bad, 60% of the film had to be changed.

588. A picture of Walt Disney appears in the orphanage.

Megamind
2010

589. The film's plot was based on the premise, "What if Lex Luthor defeated Superman?"

590. Megamind's posters say, "No you can't." This is an obvious reference to Barack Obama's slogan, "Yes we can."

591. Ben Stiller voices Bernard. He auditioned for the titular role.

592. Will Ferrel voices Megamind. The studio's first choice for the role was Robert Downey Jr.

593. Megamind's lackey, Minion, is based on the alien in the film, Robot Monster.

594. Megamind's invisible car is a parody of Batman's Batmobile and Wonder Woman's Invisible Jet.

595. The original title was Master Mind.

596. Metro Man's poses are based on Elvis. Megamind's poses are based on Alice Cooper.

597. The film was supposed to be in live-action.

598. When Megamind confronts Metro Man, he says, "Speak, apparition." This line is taken from Hamlet.

599. Megamind mispronounces 20 words throughout the film.

Minions
2015

600. A young Gru can be seen at the VillainCon. He is watching Dr. Nefario using his freeze ray gun.

601. In the original script, the Minions were genetically altered corn kernels.

602. Minions say "bi-do," which means "I'm sorry."

603. When Scarlet asks the Minions if they know who Queen Elizabeth is, Kevin answers with, "La Cucaracha." This is Spanish for "Cockroach."

604. All the tall Minions have the same hairstyle.

605. The Minions are based on the Jawas from Star Wars and the Oompa Loompas from Willie Wonka and the Chocolate Factory.

606. In the first trailer, the Minions have crooked teeth. In the second trailer, the Minions have straight teeth.

607. Despite the fact that Scarlet's surname is Overkill, she doesn't kill anyone.

608. The villain from The Smurfs, Gargamel, is in front of the Minions at VillianCon.

Moana
2016

609. Moana's grandmother is called Tala. "Tala" means "story" in Samoan.

610. Disney looked at the cowboy film, True Grit, as an inspiration for the two main characters.

611. When Maui fights, he performs a war dance called a Haka. The Maori people perform Hakas before battle.

612. When Maui meets Moana, he cocks his eyebrow. This is a signature move of Dwayne Johnson.

613. At one point, villagers can be seen beating a rug. If you look closely, you can see the rug looks the same as the magic carpet from Aladdin.

614. Maui's tattoos were not made with CGI. Instead, they were hand-drawn.

615. One of the Kakamora's is modelled on Baymax from Big Hero 6.

616. The film was meant to revolve entirely around Maui. When the filmmakers ventured to Hawaii, they fell in love with the Polynesian folklore and thought the story would be better if a mortal character learned about the legend of Maui.

617. The Kakamora scene was inspired by the chase scene in Mad Max: Fury Road.

618. This is the second time Dwayne Johnson has played a demi-god. He played the title character in Hercules.

Monsters vs. Aliens
2009

619. Most of the creatures are based on famous movie monsters. Reese Witherspoon's character, Ginormica, is based on the giant in Attack of the 50 Foot Woman. Hugh Laurie's character, Dr. Cockroach, is based on The Fly. Seth Rogen's character, BOB, is based on The Blob. Will Arnett's character, The Missing Link, is based on Creature from the Black Lagoon.

620. The tagline is, "The Weird Will Save the World."

621. The film revolves around the government using monsters for missions to take down hostile monsters. This concept is similar to the comic and movie, Hellboy. Weirdly, Jeffrey Tambor starred in both films.

622. Kiefer Sutherland voices WR Monger. His name is an obvious reference to the word, "warmonger."

623. WR Monger's insignia is based on Shrek's face.

624. This was the first animated film to be made in 3D. Every other film prior to this one was made in 2D and then converted into 3D.

625. The story is set in Modesto. This is the birthplace of George Lucas.

626. The song that the president plays on the synthesiser is the theme song from Beverly Hills Cop.

627. John Krasinksi voices Cuthbert. Ed Helms voices the News Reporter. Rainn Wilson voices the villain Gallaxhar. All these actors starred in the US version of The Office.

Mr. Peabody & Sherman
2014

628. Mr. Peabody originally appeared in the 1950s animated series, The Adventures of Rocky and Bullwinkle and Friends. His segments were known as Peabody's Improbably History.

629. Peabody is the world's smartest dog. He is so intelligent, he becomes bored with his life and decides to adopt a human child called Sherman. To entertain and educate Sherman, Peabody builds a time-machine and travels to pivotal moments in history.

630. Although Robert Downey Jr was cast as Peabody, he dropped out as he was too busy to commit to the role. Ty Burrell was then cast as Peabody.

631. The time-machine is called the WABAC, which is an abbreviation of Wavelength Acceleration Bi-directional Asynchronus Controller.

632. The WABAC travels at 88mph. This is the same speed the DeLorean travels in Back to the Future to travel through time.

633. The film spawned an animated series in 2015 called The Mr. Peabody & Sherman Show.

634. Peabody is an inventor, scientist, Nobel laureate, and a two-time Olympic medallist.

635. The film was supposed to come out in 2003.

636. The film was directed by Rob Minkoff. Minkoff directed The Lion King.

Nausicaa of the Valley of the Wind
1984

637. This film was released in 1984. Shia LeBeouf (who was born in 1986) voices Asbel in the 2005 English dub. This means that Shia is credited for the film even though he wasn't born until after the film was originally released.

638. The film was heavily re-edited and released worldwide in 1985 as "Warriors of the Wind." The director, Hayao Miyazaki, was so upset about this cut that when a producer wanted to edit Miyazaki's film, Princess Mononoke, Miyazaki sent him a sword with the words, "NO CUTS" written on it.

639. Because it was directed by Miyazaki, many fans assume that this a Studio Ghibli film. However, the film was made before Studio Ghibli was formed.

640. Miyazaki was worried the film wouldn't sell because it wasn't based on any book or merchandise. To counter this, he created a comic based on the story to promote the film.

641. The military planes are based on the Nazi Luftwaffe.

642. The female is called Oh-Baba. Her name means "great old woman."

643. Nausicaa's glider is called Mehve. "Mehve" is German for "seagull."

644. The name "Nausicaa" comes from a character in Homer's The Odyssey.

The Nightmare Before Christmas
1993

645. In the opening scene, you can see that the bats are on wires. This movie is stop-motioned so the wires are completely unnecessary. They were put in as a reference to the awful special effects from old horror movies.

646. 400 heads were made for Jack Skellington.

647. Vincent Price was cast as Santa Claus. Sadly, he died before he could complete his lines.

648. If a single frame was out of place, the animators had to reshoot an entire scene.

649. The film cost $18 million. It made $75 million at the box office.

650. The film was nearly made in 1982.

651. There are 60 characters in the film.

652. Up to four puppets were made for each character.

653. The director wanted Oogie Boogie to be Dr. Finklestein in disguise. Tim Burton was so angry when he heard this idea, he kicked a hole through a wall.

654. Despite the amount of effort that was put into the puppets, only four puppeteers worked on the film.

655. It took one week to film one minute of footage.

656. Two inventions were created for the film. The light alarm was devised to warn animators if the stage lights

failed to come on. Also, a system was created so a puppeteer could switch to another puppet if their original puppet malfunctioned.

657.   Despite what many people believe, this film was directed by Henry Selick, not Tim Burton. Burton was only on set for 10 days. Ironically, the film is called Tim Burton's The Nightmare Before Christmas in certain countries.

The Pirates! Band of Misfits
2012

658. The plague ship was originally called the leper ship but the word "leper" was removed after a leprosy charity complained.

659. Most of the main cast is British. Many of the actors were replaced with Americans when the film was released in the US.

660. The original title was The Pirates! In an Adventure with Scientists! This is the title of the 2004 book that the film is based on.

661. The Irish pirate wears a Blue Peter badge.

662. The film inspired a short called So You Want to Be a Pirate!

663. The Elephant Man appears for a second in the scene where the Pirate Captain is selling baby clothes.

664. David Tennant voices Charles Darwin. Darwin meets Queen Victoria in this film. Weirdly, Tennant's character also met Queen Victoria in Doctor Who.

665. Although the film was made with stop-motion, CGI was used for the sky and sea.

666. Since the story is set in 1837, Queen Victoria should be 17.

Pocahontas
1995

667. Originally, all the animals could speak. Their dialogue was cut to make the tone more serious.

668. Pocahontas uses willow bark on John Smith after he is shot. Willow bark contains salicylic acid, which is a fundamental component in aspirin.

669. The writers considered having Pocahontas' people only speak in Powhatan.

670. Billy Connolly voices Ben.

671. John Candy was cast as Redfeather the turkey. Although he had most of his voiceover work done, the character was scrapped when Candy suddenly died.

672. Pocahontas is American. The only other American Disney princess is Tiana from the 2009 film, The Princess and the Frog.

673. Colours of the Wind won an Oscar for Best Song. The film won another Oscar for Best Music Score.

674. Sean Bean was considered for John Smith. The role went to Mel Gibson.

675. Jeffrey Katzenberg was the studio head of Disney at the time of this film's release. He was so proud of Pocahontas that he thought it would be Oscar-nominated for Best Film.

676. Many sources incorrectly state that this film is a flop. It cost $55 million and made $346 million at the box office.

Pokémon: The First Movie
Mewtwo Strikes Back
1998

677. This film had the highest-grossing opening for an animated film in history. However, the film lost that title two weeks later to Toy Story 2.

678. Since Mewtwo is psychic, he doesn't speak since he can project his thoughts into people's minds. The animators were relieved by this since they had great difficulty matching up the lip movements of each character when they spoke.

679. The Japanese version has a completely different story.

680. Dragonite has a purse. The director joked that he hoped this would make male purses come back in style.

681. In the Japanese version, Mewtwo is perceived in a more sympathetic light since he sees himself as an outsider who simply wants to belong in the world. In the American version, Mewtwo is an evil tyrant who wishes to control the world.

682. This story was originally going to be the finale for the animated series.

683. The main characters make a huge speech at the end explaining how "fighting is wrong." Many fans found this speech illogical since the entire premise of Pokémon is to battle each other. Every single episode of the Pokémon animated series has a Pokémon battle.

684. The film spawned over 20 sequels.

The Prince of Egypt
1998

685. The film takes place in 1200 BC.

686. At the time, it was the most expensive animated film ever, costing $70 million. It made over $218 million at the box office.

687. This was co-directed by Brenda Chapman. She was the first female to a major animated feature. She also co-directed the film, Brave.

688. The film was sent to theatres under the codename "Edgar Allen. This name is based on the poet, Edgar Allen Poe. "POE" is the initials of "Prince of Egypt."

689. A shadow can be seen in the Red Sea after it has risen. Many viewers assume the shadow is of a whale. It is actually of a Megalodon shark; the largest shark to ever exist.

690. The song, When You Believe, won an Oscar.

691. This film was banned in Malaysia and Indonesia.

692. The Red Sea parting scene required ten animators and took two years to animate.

693. The final plague kills every firstborn child apart from those who have marked their doors with lamb's blood. The constellation of Orion is visible when the final plague takes place. Orion was a gigantic huntsman in Greek mythology who hunted for his god, Zeus. This constellation seems applicable to the scene as a godly spirit is hunting down the first-born children.

Ralph Breaks the Internet
2018

694. Ralph and Vanellope were meant to meet the Disney princesses in the video game, Disney Infinity.

695. Mindy Kaling is the only actor to appear in the previous film that was recast for Ralph Breaks the Internet. Although she played Taffyta in Wreck-It Ralph, she was replaced with Melissa Villasenor. It is unknown what Kaling didn't return for the role.

696. The video game, Slaughter Race, is based on the 1995 franchise, Twisted Metal.

697. Gal Gadot voices Shank. The character is based on the Fast and the Furious character, Gisele, who Gadot also played.

698. Litwak's Arcade is situated in Los Aburridos. "Aburrido" is Spanish for "boring."

699. When Ralph enters the OlderNet, he crosses a Y2K survival kit.

700. The film received criticism as Moana's skin colour appears lighter than in her original film.

701. The film cost $175 million. It made $526 million at the box office.

702. One of the Stormtroopers from Star Wars performs a Wilhelm Scream. This sound effect is used in every Star Wars film and is the most famous scream in movie history.

703. Weirdly, this film and the previous one came out the same year as a Dr. Seuss adaptation. Wreck-It Ralph came out the same year as The Lorax. This film came out the same year as The Grinch.

Rio
2011

704. Will.i.am voices Pedro.

705. The tagline is, "1 out of every 8 Americans is afraid of flying. Most of them don't have feathers."

706. Pixar cancelled their film, Newt, because the story was too similar to Rio.

707. Jesse Eisenberg voices the lead character, Blu. He recorded his lines during the weekends. During the weekdays, he worked on The Social Network. Eisenberg agreed to star in Rio as he thought it would be fun compared to The Social Network which he considered a "joyless" experience.

708. When Tulio sees his reflection while he is dressed as a macaw, he says, "Cyanopsitta Spixxi!" This is the scientific name for the Spix's macaw.

Rise of the Guardians
2012

709. Santa Claus is depicted as a Russian called North. Every time he is surprised, North shouts the name of a classic Russian composter like Shostakovich or Rimsky-Korsakov.

710. The film revolves around a league of fairy tale characters like Santa, the Easter Bunny, the Sandman, Jack Frost, and the Tooth Fairy.
    If the film did well, the director expected to make sequels with many more mythical characters. Sadly, the film only made a minor profit and the series was cancelled.

711. Chris Pine voices Jack Frost. The role was supposed to go to Leonardo DiCaprio.

712. Jack Frost calls the Easter Bunny a kangaroo. This is because Bunny's voice actor, Hugh Jackman, is Australian.

Robots
2005

713. Robots was directed by Chris Wedge. He is most famous for voicing Scrat from the Ice Ages series.

714. Robin Williams voices Fender. If Robin Williams had to do a scene ten times, he would usually try it in ten different accents.

715. Paula Abdul voices Watch.

716. Jim Broadbent voices the villain, Madame Gasket.

717. The tagline was, "Repair for adventure!"

718. This was the first animated film that Robin Williams starred in since Aladdin and the King of Thieves.

719. This was originally going to be a musical.

720. On Fender's Map of the Stars Homes, it reads – Jeremy Iron, Orson Wheels, Axle Roses, Britney Gears, Farrah Faucet, and MC Hammer.

The Secret of NIMH
1982

721. The film is based on the novel, Mrs. Frisby and the Rats of NIMH. It was written by Robert C. O'Brien in 1971.

722. In the novel, the main character is called Brisby, not Frisby. Her name was changed to avoid legal ramifications from the Frisbee company, Wham-O.

723. The director was Don Bluth. He left Disney to make this film. It was rejected by Disney for being "too dark." After it did well, 20 Disney animators left the company. They were known as the Disney Defectors.

724. The dragonfly that Mr. Ages chases is Evinrude; the same dragonfly from The Rescuers.

725. Renowned thespian, Derek Jacobi, voices Nicodemus.

726. Will Wheaton voices Martin. This was his film debut. He is best-known for playing Wesley in Star Trek: The Next Generation.

727. The sword fight at the end was almost entirely copied from the climactic scene in The Adventures of Robin Hood.

728. The film cost $7 million. At the time, this was the most expensive animated film that was not made by Disney.

729. The film has many supernatural elements. These aspects do not exist in the original novel.

Shark Tale
2004

730. Many of the products have a fish-pun name e.g. Coral Cola (Coca-Cola,) Newsreef (Newsweek,) Old Wavy (Old Navy,) Gup (GAP,) etc.

731. The title was going to be Sharkslayer but the CEO changed it at the last minute, worried that it sounded too scary.

732. Ziggy Marley voices Ernie the Jellyfish. Ziggy is Bob Marley's son.

733. Will Smith voices Oscar. The animators made Oscar's ears stick out like Smith's do in real life.

734. When Oscar goes to the clock, there's a note on the wall that reads, "If you don't come in Saturday, don't bother." The CEO, Jeffrey Katzenberg, infamously sent this memo to executives while he was in charge of Disney.

735. The story is very similar to the 1897 tale, The Reluctant Dragon, which was written by Kenneth Grahame. Grahame is best-known for writing The Wind in the Willows.

736. Robert De Niro voices Don Lino. Like De Niro, Don Lino has a mole on his cheek.

Shaun the Sheep Movie
2015

737. It took six years to make this film.

738. The stop-motion animation was so painstaking, the animators could only produce two seconds of footage per day.

739. 20 animators worked on this film.

740. Although there are 17 voice actors, there is no dialogue whatsoever.

741. It was released on the Chinese New Year's Day. This is the Year of the Sheep.

742. One of the cat's in Animal Control has a mask like Hannibal Lecter.

743. The tagline was, "Catch them if ewe can!"

744. Shaun's bag has a Blue Peter badge.

745. The Farmer's farm is called Mossy Bottom Farm.

746. When the Farmer is called Mr. X, he poses exactly like Wolverine from the X-Men series. Wolverine is also known as Weapon X.

A Shaun the Sheep Movie: Farmageddon
2019

747. This is the first feature length sequel that Aardman ever made.

748. The crew studied the film, 2001: A Space Odyssey for certain shots in this film.

749. The first shot is a parody of the opening shot in the film, Contact.

750. There is a garage called HG Wheels. This is a reference to the writer, HG Wells. This film parodies War of the Worlds, which was written by Wells.

751. Rocky from Chicken Run cameos in one shot. He can be seen on a wall holding a coffee mug.

Shrek
2001

752. Shrek's mud shower was so hard to animate, that one of the animators had to take a mud bath to see how the mud moved.

753. Shrek has a size 22 shoe.

754. In the beginning, Papa Bear, Mama Bear, and Baby Bear can be seen in cages. In a night time scene, Papa Bear is comforting Baby Bear. In a later scene, a rug of Mama Bear can be seen in Farquad's castle.

755. The villain, Lord Farquaad, is based on the former Disney CEO, Michael Eisner.

756. The Duloc jingle is a parody of Disney's It's A Small World After All. DreamWorks' lawyers were worried that Disney would sue them over the song.

757. When Fiona asks Shrek and Donkey about Lord Farquaad, they mock his height. However, when they met Farquaad, there was no way that Shrek and Donkey could see that he was a dwarf.

758. Everything in Farquaad's castle is angular. Nothing has curves or bends.

759. Farquaad's logo is similar to the Facebook logo.

760. As the creators were putting the finishing touches on the film, they realised that they skipped Shrek's line, "What are you doing in my swamp?" The producer had to track down Mike Myers and record him saying this line for the sake of continuity.

761. In the 1940 film, Pinocchio, naughty boys are turned into donkeys on Pleasure Island.

There is an Internet theory that Donkey in this film is one of these boys. This seems possible since Pinocchio exists in this world as well. On top of that, Donkey is one of the only characters that doesn't seem to fit with any other fairy-tale.

Shrek 2
2004

762. One of the signs in The Poison Apple bar reads, No one under XXI admitted."

763. While Puss is in the pub, he says, "I hate Mondays." This is a reference to feline character, Garfield, who is known for hating Mondays.

764. Antonio Banderas had to record the hairball scene for three hours. He damaged his voice during the recording so much, it effected his voice for months.

    Shortly after his recording, he performed the Broadway show, 9. However, the octave range for the musical was lowered because his voice was so strained.

765. Originally, King Harold was a nudist.

766. When Gingy is watching Knights, the police say that they have spotted Shrek on a "white bronco." This scene is based on the chase in 1994 when police were tracking OJ Simpson who was driving a white Bronco.

767. The animators had difficulty making the hair of female characters look realistic. They were struggling so much, a wig weaver visited DreamWorks studio to explain how he makes hair look realistic.

768. At one point, the Fairy Godmother says, "What in Grimm's name?" This is a reference to the Brother's Grimm who compiled many classic fairy-tales like Snow White, Cinderella, and Sleeping Beauty.

769. Gingy lost his leg in the last film. In this film, he had his limb re-attached with frosting.

770. The developers started working on this film before the first film was even finished.

771. The entrance to Far Far Away is similar to the entrance of Paramount Studios.

The Simpsons Movie
2007

772. Moe's Tavern is called Moe's Bar in the film.

773. Only one joke from the first draft made it into the final cut.

774. The film cost $75 million. It made $527 million at the box office.

775. Albert Brooks plays the villain, Russ Cargill. He is best-known for voicing Marlin in Finding Nemo.

776. The villain was supposed to be Hank Scorpio. Scorpio was also voiced by Albert Brooks.

777. Homer jumps over the gorge at the end of the film. This is an obvious reference to when Homer attempted to jump the gorge in The Simpsons episode, Bart the Daredevil. After Homer fails the jump, he is put into an ambulance. The ambulance immediately crashes into a tree, and Homer falls out and tumbles off the gorge again.

    In this film, you can see the crashed ambulance is still embedded into the tree.

778. The film was made by David Silverman. He co-directed Monsters, Inc.

779. Halfway through the film, the Simpsons move to Alaska. Weirdly, there is a city in Alaska called Homer.

780. When the Simpsons enter Alaska, the border guard gives them $1000. Alaska actually does this but only if the citizen resides there for at least a year.

Sinbad:
Legend of the Seven Seas
2003

781. Brad Pitt voices Sinbad. Catherine Zeta-Jones voices Marina. They didn't meet until the film premiered.

782. In this story, Sinbad is Greek. In the original story, he is a Muslim from Iraq.

783. Russel Crowe was the first choice for Sinbad.

784. Michelle Pfeifer voices the villain, Eris. She accepted the role after her children begged her to.

785. Sinbad's dog, Spike, was so popular in test-screenings, the filmmakers added in seven more scenes with him.

Sleeping Beauty
1959

786. Aurora is barefoot in every scene except the finale.

787. Although there are many versions of Sleeping Beauty, the film is mainly based on the Grimm version.

788. Aurora and Philip dance in the clouds. This shot was nearly used for Snow White and the Seven Dwarfs.

789. The clouds above Maleficent's castle are skull-shaped.

790. Although it came out in 1959, Sleeping Beauty wasn't released on video until 1986.

791. Eleanor Audley voices Maleficent. She also voices Lady Tremaine in Cinderella, Betty Rubble in The Flintstones, and Granny in The Looney Tunes cartoons.

792. Mary Costa voices Aurora. Walt Disney intentionally never met her until the production ended, worried that her appearance and personality might cause him to alter the character.

793. Costa became an incredibly successful singer after the release of this film. She went on to appear in 44 operas and even sang at John F. Kennedy's funeral.

794. Maleficent's look is based on Morticia from The Addams' Family. Her head's shape is based on a bat.

795. The animation of Maleficent calling upon thunderclouds is taken from the final scene in Fantasia.

796. Sleeping Beauty was the most successful film of the year apart from Ben-Hur.

797. The film cost $6 million, making it the most expensive Disney animation at the time. Although the film made a lot of money, it wasn't considered a success as it cost so much to make.

Walt Disney was in so much debt by the time the film premiered, he was forced to slash his animation personnel from 551 to 75 within a year.

Smallfoot
2018

798. The story revolves around a group of mythical creatures (yetis) who are terrified of humans. This is the basis for the story of Monsters Inc. and Hotel Transylvania.

799. The main male and female characters are Migo and Meechee. These are two different Tibetan words for "yeti."

800. The screaming goat is based on the popular YouTube videos of goats unconventionally screaming.

801. The yetis hear the humans speak in a high-pitched squeaking sound. These noises were provided by the film's editor.

802. In the UK version, Mama Bear is voiced by Spice Girl singer, Emma Bunton.

Smurfs:
The Lost Village
2017

803. The live-action film, The Smurfs, was released in 2011. The Smurfs 2 was released in 2013. Since they didn't make a lot of money, the studio decided to reboot the franchise as an animated film.

    The only actor who reprised his role from the live-action film is Frank Welker who provides the voice of Gargamel's cat, Azrael.

804. Julia Roberts voices SmurfWillow.

805. Jonathan Winters provided the voice for Papa Smurf in the live-action films. He was replaced by Mandy Patinkin in this film. The role nearly went to John Goodman.

806. The tagline was, "Small is big..." That doesn't even make sense.

807. The title was meant to be Get Smurfy.

808. The film was delayed by two years.

809. Ryan Reynolds was considered for the role of Clumsy.

810. Taylor Swift auditioned for Smurfette.

811. Mike Myers really wanted to voice Brainy Smurf. When he saw the film, Myers said he hated it.

812. This is the first time that Gordon Ramsay played a character in a film that wasn't based on himself.

Snow White and the Seven Dwarfs
1937

813. Ward Kimball nearly quit the production after two scenes that he animated were cut. Disney made it up to him by letting him animate Jiminy Cricket in Pinocchio.

814. Snow White is the youngest human Disney princess. She is only 14 years old.

815. Walt Disney attended the premier of this film. He didn't attend another premier until Mary Poppins.

816. Walt Disney considered a sequel.

817. Dopey was supposed to be voiced by Mel Blanc. Blanc voices Bugs Bunny and is considered to be the best voice actor ever.

818. Happy is the only dwarf that Snow White doesn't refer to by name.

819. The initial budget was $250,000. In the end, the film cost $1.5 million, which was a huge amount for the time. It made over $184 million at the box office, which was four times more than any other film that year. It was the most successful film ever at the time.

    Sadly, it only held onto that record for the year when it was eclipsed by Gone with the Wind in 1939.

820. The film won a special Oscar that consisted of a regular Oscar and seven miniature statuettes.

821. The dwarves say "Jiminy Crickets" at two points in the film. Jiminy Cricket appeared in Pinocchio.

822. Despite the fact that the dwarves mine diamonds every day, there is no explanation with what they do with the diamonds or why the dwarves aren't rich.

823. There is an Internet rumour that "Prince Charming" is actually Death and he is taking Snow White to Heaven... that's a bit dark.

824. Lucilla La Verne voices the Evil Queen. The first time she performed the Old Witch voice, the animators were astounded by how different she sounded. When they asked her how she did that voice. La Verne said, "Oh, I just took my teeth out."

Spirited Away
2001

825. Bizarrely, the film didn't have a script. The director showed the whole story to the cast and crew through storyboards. He does this for all his films.

826. Haku's name translates into "God of the Swift Amber River."

827. While in his dragon form, Haku's movements are based on a gecko and a snake.

828. After Chihiro leaves the Spirit World, she loses all memory of her time there.

829. Originally No Face had green hair and a very large mouth on his chest.

830. The director said the hardest thing about the movie was cutting scenes. If he kept every scene in the finished film, it would've been three hours long.

831. Studio Ghibli studied the behaviour of their daughters to make Chihiro's behaviour as accurate as possible. When her parents ask her a question, she doesn't answer until they ask a second time because the crew's daughters were easily distracted. Also, when Chihiro puts her shoes on, she taps them into the ground to make them fit properly.

832. The executive producer of Pixar, John Lasseter, supervised this film.

833. This is the first film ever to earn $200 million before being released in the US.

Spirit:
Stallion of the Cimarron
2002

834. The story revolves a wild horse captured by humans. One of the actors is called Mike Horse.

835. Spirit was modelled after a three-year-old stallion called Donner.

836. It's common practise to have actors imitate animal voices for cats, dogs, horses, etc. for an animated film. To make the film more authentic, real stallions were used for all the horse sounds.

837. The clouds in the opening scene are designed to resemble running horses.

838. Tom Hanks was considered for the narrator.

The SpongeBob SquarePants Movie
2004

839. The film was supposed to be the show's series finale.

840. The trailer used footage from the films, Das Boot, The Hunt for Red October, and U-571.

841. Scarlet Johansson voices Mindy.

842. Alec Baldwin voices Dennis.

843. The tagline was "Bigger, squarier, spongier!"

**The SpongeBob Movie:
Sponge Out of Water**
2015

844. Pearl only talks during the credits.

845. Although Slash from Guns N' Roses appears in the trailer and a deleted scene, he was absent from the film.

846. This film is not be a direct sequel to the last SpongeBob movie. It exists in its own continuity.

847. SpongeBob creator, Stephen Hillenburg voices the stroller baby that cries, "SpongeBob!"

848. The vortex that Plankton and SpongeBob pass through is based on the wormhole in 2001: A Space Odyssey.

The SpongeBob SquarePants Movie: Sponge on the Run
2020

849. The working title was It's A Wonderful Sponge.

850. The story is based on the episode, Have You Seen This Snail?

851. The film was delayed by a year.

852. The previous film inspired a mobile game called Sponge on the Run, which is the title of this film.

Street Fighter II:
The Animated Movie
1994

853. When Chun Li reveals data about Shadowlaw, Balrog is referred to as Bison.

854. According to the cyborg's database, Chun Li's master is called B. Lee. This is a reference to Bruce Lee.

855. The director made a prequel animated series, Street Fighter II: V. It also spawned a prequel film in 1999 called Street Fighter Alpha.

856. Steve Blum voices T. Hawk. Although many people may not recognise his name, he is considered to be one of the best voice actors ever and has over 600 acting credits.

857. Akuma cameos for a second in the scene where Ryu visits India. Akuma is a secret character in the Street Fighter video game series.

858. Bison's terrorist group is called Shadowlaw. In the video games, it's called Shadaloo.

859. Many elements from the movie were incorporated into the video game including Bison's scientist, the Shadowlaw jet, Ken's long hair, etc.

860. Bryan Cranston voices Fei Long. Cranston is best-known for playing Walter White in Breaking Bad.
    According to the credits, Fei Long is voiced by "Phil Williams" due to voice actor union legalities.

The Sword in the Stone
1963

861. Merlin's crankiness and playful manner were based on Walt Disney. Merlin even has the same nose as Walt. Walt didn't know this until the film was released.

862. Three actors voice Arthur.

863. The short, Winnie the Pooh and a Day for Eeyore, was shown in the cinema before this film.

864. This was the first Disney film to be made by a single director.

865. Apart from the prologue, Excalibur doesn't appear for 71 minutes. The film is only 79 minutes long.

866. The film concludes with a battle between Merlin and Mad Madam Mim. They attack each other by transforming into several different animals.

Most animators say this scene is one of the most significant scenes in animated history. In fact, many new animators study this scene to see how to animate a creature but maintain its character with easily definable features. Every animal that Merlin turns into looks gentle and every animal that Mim turns into looks evil.

Tangled
2010

867. Mandy Moore voices Rapunzel. The role nearly went to Natalie Portman or Reese Witherspoon.

868. Rapunzel's first song was nearly cut from the film.

869. The film spawned a 2D show called Tangled: The Series in 2017.

870. Maximus uses a Roman gladius sword. This blade seems fitting since Maximus is a Roman name.

871. Pascal is a chameleon. He was supposed to be a squirrel.

872. The Stabbingtons are called Patchy and Not-Patchy.

873. Richard Kiel voices Vlad. Kiel is best-known for playing Jaws in the James Bond series.

874. Pascal was modelled after the producer's chameleon.

875. The film spawned a six-minute short in 2012 called Tangled Ever After.

876. It's a well-known fact that Rapunzel and Flynn cameo at the beginning of Frozen. Weirdly, the directors of Tangled had no idea that the characters were going to appear in the film until it was released.

877. Zachary Levi voices Flynn. He auditioned for the role in a British accent. He uses an American accent for the film.

878. The first scene to be completed was the interrogation between Rapunzel and Flynn.

879. Rapunzel is always barefoot to represent her innocence. The actress, Mandy Moore, was barefoot while recording her lines.

880. The spinning wheel from Sleeping Beauty is in the tower.

881. The film was made in two years. By comparison, most Disney films take four years to make. Bizarrely, the last 60% of the animation was completed in the last two months.

882. Rapunzel is the first green-eyed Disney princess.

883. Gothel only shows her love to Rapunzel's hair, not Rapunzel herself. She only kisses Rapunzel on her hair and strokes her hair when she acts affectionately to Rapunzel. Gothel calls her "my little flower," which is a reference to the sunflower that keeps Gothel young.

When Flynn shows affection to Rapunzel, he pushes her hair away so he can see her face clearly.

Tarzan
1999

884. Some of the filmmakers went to Uganda to watch gorillas in their natural environment. Although they assumed the apes would be ferocious, the crew were surprised how calm and peaceful the gorillas were.

885. At one point, a baboon eats a papaya, even though this fruit is indigenous to South America.

886. Most gorilla sounds are actually from chimps because the gorilla noises sounded too aggressive.

887. In the original story, Tarzan was adopted by a fictional ape called a Mangani. This ape resembled a chimp, not a gorilla.

888. Brendan Fraser auditioned for the role of Tarzan. He went on to play a parody of the character in the film, George of the Jungle.

889. In the final scene, Tarzan was supposed to go to England as a civilized man.

890. Phil Collins performed the movie's song in five different languages.

891. The film spawned a sequel in 2002 called Tarzan & Jane that takes place a year after the pair get married.

892. This is considered the last film of the Disney Renaissance.

893. Phil Collins won an Oscar for his song, You'll Be in My Heart. Disney didn't win an Oscar for another animated film until 2013 for Frozen.

TMNT
2007

894. Leonardo, Raphael, and Donatello have brown eyes. Michelangelo was given blue eyes to make him appear younger and more innocent.

895. Some of the monsters are based on mythological beasts including the Yeti, the Cyclops, a gargoyle, and the Jersey Devil.

896. Mako voices Splinter. Although he is not well-known in the Western world, he has a cult following and is considered to be one of the most respectable actors in Japanese cinema. He died a year before the film was released.

    It was publicly announced that Mako would star in the film the day before he died.

897. Sarah Michelle Gellar voices April O' Neill.

898. Raphael died in the original script.

899. Renowned director, Kevin Smith, voices the Diner Cook.

900. The Japanese lullaby that Splinter sings was ad-libbed by Mako.

901. Chris Evans voices Casey Jones. Chris Evans has played five comic book characters; Casey Jones in this film, the Human Torch in Fantastic Four, Jensen in The Losers, Lucas Lee in Scott Pilgrim vs the World, and Captain America in the Marvel Cinematic Universe.

The Thief and the Cobbler
1993

902. This film was in development longer than any movie in history – 28 years.

903. Vincent Price voices ZigZag. This was the last film he made as he passed away the same year it was originally released. He recorded his dialogue 20 years before the film was released.

904. The film was originally made by Richard Williams. In 1988, Warner Bros took over the production. When Aladdin was released in 1992, Warner Bros. thought The Thief and the Cobbler's story was too similar so the studio abandoned this film.

    It was then picked up by a producer called Fred Calvert. Calvert kicked Williams off the project and retitled the film as The Princess and the Cobbler. This version was released in 1993 in Australia and South Africa.

    This version was considered disastrous and so, was heavily re-edited with new animations and voice actors by Miramax Films. It was then released in North America under the title, Arabian Knight, in 1995.

905. The film cost $28 million. It made a pitiful $319,723 at the box office.

906. The uncut version has the most onscreen deaths in movie history – over a thousand.

907. Sean Connery was meant to have one line but he didn't show up for the recording.

908. The director, Richard Williams, got a bunch of Irish people drunk for the Brigands scene. The actors got so

drunk, they ended up fighting each other. The fight was recorded and used for the film.

909. Richard Williams was so devastated by the film's failure that he refuses to talk about it. When he attends lectures, he has bodyguards that will remove anyone who mentions The Thief and the Cobbler.

910. Williams has never seen the Calvert or Miramax cut. His son watched it and told Williams that "If I ever want to jump off a bridge then I should take a look."

911. The film wasn't released in the UK until 2012.

912. The director created the animation for the film, Who Framed Roger Rabbit.

The Three Caballeros
1944

913. The film revolves around Donald Duck's adventures with a Brazilian parrot called Jose Carioca and a Mexican rooster called Panchito Pistoles. The film was only made to improve the US' relationship with South America during World War II.

914. This was the last animated Disney to be released during World War II.

915. "Caballero" means "gentleman" in Spanish.

916. The film was made alongside the 42-minute animated short, Saludos Amigos. Like The Three Caballeros, Saludos Amigos was only made to improve the relationship between North and South America.

917. This is considered to be the most obscure animated Disney film. Many die-hard Disney fans are oblivious to its existence.

918. Many people assume Pistoles surname is Spanish for "pistols". However, the Spanish for pistols is "pistolas."

919. Although the film never had a sequel, the three main characters appeared in the 1948 film, Melody Time.

Toy Story
1995

920. Woody is seen as an old-school toy who is replaced with revolutionary "cool" toy, Buzz Lightyear. The director based this concept on his childhood experience. As a kid, he loved his Casper doll but threw it away when the new "cool" toy came out; GI Joe.

921. Pizza Planet was originally called Pizza Putt and would've been a mini-golf pizzeria. This was changed into a space-themed pizzeria so Buzz would believe he was reaching Star Command.

922. Originally, the film was going to revolve a toy called Tinny. Tinny was the main character in 1988 animated short, Tin Toy.

923. In Andy's room, there are books on the shelf called Tin Toy, Knick Knack, Red's Dream and Luxo Jr. These are the names of animated shorts made by Pixar in the 1980s.

924. Tom Hanks agreed to the role of Woody because he wondered if his toys were alive when he was a kid.

925. When Woody dunks his head into a bowl of cereal, no milk spills out because the animators couldn't animate liquid properly at the time.

926. Laurie Metcalf voices Andy's Mom. She is best-known for playing Jackie Harris in the TV series, Roseanne, and Mary Cooper in The Big Band Theory.

927. The film was nearly a musical.

928. Despite the film's legacy, it didn't win a single Oscar apart from an Honorary Award.

929. The director pitched the film to the studio by saying, "What if your toy was looking for you as hard as you were looking for it?"

930. The animators bought tons of toys and took them apart to see how to make them move accurately.

931. Bo Peep's appearance in the film references Hans Christian Andersen's fairy tale, The Shepherdess and the Sweep. In this story, toys come to life when children don't look at them.

Toy Story 2
1999

932. Wheezy is based on Linux's mascot, Tux.

933. Jim Varney voices Slinky. He died three months after the film was released.

934. When Al hangs up the phone with a Japanese businessman, he says, "Don't touch my moustache." This is a mnemonical joke because "Don't touch my moustache." sounds like the Japanese for "You're welcome."

935. 90% of the film was deleted by accident! Luckily, the technical director made a copy of the film (without anyone's permission) to show to her kids. When the film was deleted, she had the only copy.

  When it was brought into the office, the animators said that they only lost a week of work. If she didn't make a copy, it's very likely that the film would have never been made.

936. Jessie tells Woody how she was abandoned in the song, When She Loved Me. Pixar were worried that a three-minute song about love would bore children.

937. After Woody has a nightmare, the toys can be seen playing cards. All the cards are the Ace of spades. In fortune telling, this card represents death.

938. The old man that fixes Woody's arm is called Geri. He was in the Pixar short, Geri's Game.

939. The canyon that Buzz flies through was created for A Bug's Life but it was never used.

940. Over the years, a rumour circulated the Internet suggesting that Jessie's owner is actually Andy's mom. The director confirmed that this is true.

Toy Story 3
2010

941. John Lasseter directed the previous two Toy Story films. He let Lee Unkrich direct this film as he wanted to direct Cars 2.

942. The film concludes with a shot of clouds that look exactly like Andy's bedroom wallpaper in the first film.

943. The villain is a teddy bear. Pixar wanted to make a film with a villainous teddy since 1990.

944. This is the only film where Andy says the names of his toys.

945. Don Rickles voices Mr. Potato Head. Some reports state that this was the last film he worked on before he died. However, he voiced Frog in Zookeeper which came out a year after this film.

946. The film cost $200 million. Toy Story 3 made over a billion dollars at the box office, making it the most successful film of 2010.

947. The reason Bo Peep was removed was because the film concludes in an incinerator and she would have melted since she is made of porcelain.

Toy Story 4
2019

948. The keys in the antique store are based on the keys from the Disney game, Kingdom Hearts III.

949. The old toys that Bonnie doesn't play with anymore are played by old-time actors, Mel Brooks, Carl Reiner, Betty White, and Carol Burnett. Pixar cast actors who were in their prime in the 70s and 80s to highlight they are "over-the-hill" since Bonnie doesn't play with them anymore.

950. Since Annie Potts played Bo Peep in two Toy Story films before, she was aware that a very small amount of what she records will make it into the final film. Since Potts didn't have a complete script, she had absolutely no idea how large her role was until she saw the film.

951. Miguel's guitar from Coco can be won as a prize in the same carnival attraction that Bunny and Ducky live in.

952. Toy Story 4 came out the same day as Child's Play. By a freakish coincidence, both films revolve around a sentient toy who belonged to a boy called Andy.

953. Don Rickles died before he had a chance to reprise his role as Mr. Potato Head. Instead of recasting him the crew looked at all of Rickles material over the years and repurposed some of it as his dialogue for this film.

954. The film stars Keanu Reeves, Keegan-Michael Key, and Jordan Peele. All three actors starred in Keanu.

955. Many people were upset when the film was announced as fans believed the ending of Toy Story 3

was a perfect conclusion to the trilogy. The writers agreed and said they would never make a sequel unless it was as good as Toy Story 3.

956. Duke Caboom first appeared in Incredibles 2 as one of Jack-Jack's toys.

957. When Woody reunites with Bo, her sheep bring a Grape Soda cap. This is the same cap that Ellie pinned on Carl's shirt in Up.

958. When Duke Caboom is talking about himself, the Canadian National Anthem can be heard in the background.

959. Like his character, Keanu Reeves rides a motorcycle and has his own company that designs custom motorcycles.

960. Gabby Gabby is a reference to the 1960s doll, Chatty Cathy. She is also based on Talking Tina from The Twilight Zone episode, Living Doll.

961. The last thing Keanu Reeve's character says is, "Whoa." This is a reference to Reeves' character, Ted in the film, Bill & Ted's Excellent Adventure. In that film, Ted regularly says "Whoa" anytime he sees something cool.

Up
2009

962. The French short film, Above Then Beyond, revolves around an old woman who turns her house into a hot air balloon to avoid eviction.

    Since this short was released three years before Up, some people believe that this film is a rip-off of Above Then Beyond. However, this is impossible since Up began production one year before Above Then Beyond was released.

963. 20,622 balloons are used to lift Carl's house. It would take 12,658,392 balloons to lift Carl's house in real life.

964. Elie Docter voices Ellie. She is the director's daughter.

965. Christopher Plummer voices Muntz.

966. Carl is 78 years old.

967. The film cost $175 million. It made $735 million at the box office.

968. The intro is considered to be the saddest movement in Pixar history. Even when the filmmakers were looking at the storyboard, some crewmembers started crying.

969. The film won an Oscar for Best Original Score and Best Animated Feature.

970. The DVD includes the short, Dug's Special Mission.

Wallace and Gromit:
Curse of the Were-Rabbit
2005

971. 44lbs of glue had to be used every month to keep the sets stuck down.

972. 43 versions of Gromit and 35 versions of Wallace had to be created for the film.

973. Comedian, Peter Kay, voices PC Mackintosh.

974. Lady Tottington's design changed 40 times.

975. The water was created with CGI, not stop-motion.

976. Peter Sallis voices Wallace. He has voiced the character since his first appearance in the 1989 short, A Grand Day Out. DreamWorks wanted Wallace to be voiced by a famous actor that American audiences would recognise.

    The company refused, believing that nobody could voice Wallace apart from Sallis.

977. New eyes had to be made for each character every two months.

978. The Were-Rabbit model broke three times in the final scene.

979. The directors jokingly call The Curse of the Were-Rabbit "the world's first vegetarian horror film."

980. Ray Harryhausen visited the set. He is the greatest stop-motion director of all time.

WALL-E
2008

981. The Axiom's paths are color-coded; the blue ones are for humans, the white ones are for robots, and the red ones are for stewards.

982. The tagline was, "In Space, No One Can Hear You Clean."

983. One of the programmers, Justin Wright, died of a heart attack while working on the film. He was only 27 years old. The film is dedicated to him.

984. Most Pixar films require 75,000 storyboards. This film needed 125,000.

985. The person who designed EVE also designed the iPhone and the iPod.

986. Twinkies and cockroaches can be seen throughout the film. This is a reference to the myth that Twinkies and cockroaches can survive any apocalyptic scenario.

987. The DVD has a short called BURN-E that shows the adventures of a robot on the Axiom.

988. WALL-E makes skyscrapers out of trash. It takes 95 years for him to build one of these skyscrapers.

989. The Pixar team had to watch every Charlie Chaplin and Buster Keaton film every day during lunch for 18 months. This was to help them tell a story without dialogue.

990. WALL-E's name is a reference to Walt Disney. His full name is Walter Elias Disney.

Zootopia
2016

991.   Clawhauser is based on Jerry from the comedy, Parks and Recreation.

992.   Shakira voices Gazelle.

993.   There are many sight gags including the cereal, Lucky Chomps (Lucky Charms,) Lemming Bros. Bank (Lehman Bros.,) Zoogle (Google,) Pawpsicle (Popsicle,) and MuzzelTime (FaceTime.)

994.   Every sheep has rectangular pupils except Bellwether.

995.   Wolford is a wolf that patrols undercover as a ram. This is a reference to the phrase, "Wolf in sheep's clothing."

996.   Woolter and Jesse are parodies of Walter and Jesse from the tv series, Breaking Bad.

997.   Several musicians can be seen on Judy's music player. All their names are animal-based puns e.g. The Beagles, Gun N' Rodents, Kanine West, Mick Jaguar, Hyena Gomez, The Fur Fighter, Catty Perry, Destiny's Cub, and Ewe 2.

998.   Nick Wilde's design is based on the titular character from the 1973 film, Robin Hood.

999.   Disney animators have to work gruelling hours, which leaves them exhausted. They believe staying caffeinated is so important for their job, the man who supplies coffee for the animators, Carlos Benavides, is

credited for this film. His job title in the credits is Caffeination.

1000. Aladdin's magical lamp is on Yax's shelves.

www.ingramcontent.com/pod-product-compliance
Lightning Source LLC
Chambersburg PA
CBHW061949070426
42450CB00007BA/1103